The Sawdust Trail tegelism, starting with John the early days of Methodism in eighteenth-century England, came to the United States, and how it has emerged here again and again with rich variations to become a great tradition.

We learn about "Father" Dyer, who covered 10,000 miles of the Southwest on horseback, preaching all the way; Dwight Moody, friend of poor children; Rodney Smith, the gypsy boy; Billy Sunday, who "crept and crawled out from the university of poverty" to convert 100,000 people; Evangeline Booth, the pretty girl responsible for the tremendous growth of the Salvation Army; Daddy Grace, with his three million followers; Father Divine, founder of the worldwide Kingdom of Peace; Sister Aimee McPherson and the Foursquare Gospel; Reba Crawford, the darling of Broadway; and Billy Graham, who has made use of television to reach an unprecedented number of families.

THE *Sawdust Trail*

THE
Sawdust Trail

The Story of
American Evangelism

GORDON LANGLEY
HALL

Illustrated with Photographs

Macrae Smith Company
PHILADELPHIA

69305

Library of Congress Catalog Card Number 64-14870

MANUFACTURED IN THE UNITED STATES OF AMERICA

6406

269

H

For
NINITA BRISTOW REIS
who "sat at Sister Aimee's feet"

ACKNOWLEDGMENTS

It would be impossible to thank every individual or institution providing help with my research. The following have been especially helpful: His Grace, the Earl of Gainsborough, for permission to use the letter written by the Dowager Countess of Gainsborough to Queen Victoria; John Murray (Publishers) Ltd., for permission to use Queen Victoria's reply; Rolf K. McPherson, D.D., President, the International Church of the Foursquare Gospel (son of Aimee Semple McPherson); Father Divine and Mother Divine; Miss Dorothy Darling, secretary to Father Divine; Dr. Billy Graham; Robert O. Fern, Team Coordinator, the Billy Graham Evangelistic Association; the Library of Congress; Agnes Wright Spring, State Historian, the State Historical Society of Colorado; Alys Freeze, Head, Western History Department (and her staff), the Public Library, the City and County of Denver; the San Francisco Public Library; John T. Challoner, Historian, Oshkosh Public Library, Oshkosh, Wisconsin; Mrs. Hawes, Georgia Historical Society; Frank W. Pearsall, Director of Public Relations, the Northfield Schools, East Northfield, Mass.; the British Museum; George Freedly, the New York Public Library; Virginia Rugheimer (Librarian) and Minnie Pringle Haigh; the Charleston Library Society, Charleston, S. C.; N. E. S. Norris, F. S. A., Curator and Assistant Secretary, Sussex Archaeological Society; Samuel Gaillard Stoney, Historian; Mrs. W. R. Moody, East Northfield, Massachusetts; Major Andrew S. Miller, of the Salvation

Army; Mrs. Roy B. (Brownie) Adams; Rheba Crawford; Ninita Bristow Reis, for her memories of Aimee Semple McPherson; Bob Jones University, Greenville, S. C.; Patience Ross, for valuable research in England; Osyth Leeston; Joseph Rotwein; Helena Hall; Salome Bridger; M. B. Waldron, Peter Manigault, President of the *News and Courier*, Charleston, for allowing me the use of the newspaper library; Inglis Fletcher; Eli and Ethel Cornford; Barbara Aytes; the Reverend Dr. Charles Howard Graf, rector of St. John's-in-the-Village, New York City; Joyce Glover, antiquarian bookseller, Eastbourne, England; Maude E. Griffin, journalist and historian; my great-aunts Sarah Kate Ashdown and Cicely Ticehurst; Ivy Nias; Millicent Thompson; Marian Wefer; Kenneth Terrence Weller; Joseph A. Scaltro; Marion L. Foster; my secretaries Theo Frazier and Gladys McNerney (U.S.A.) and Anne Grouch (England); my typist Gertrude Young; Robert Sefton; Burton G. Harriott; Nancy O. Base and Freyda Rosamanda Stanton.

Gordon Langley Hall

TARA
1964

CONTENTS

The harvest is past, the summer is ended, and we are not saved.

JEREMIAH, Chapter 9, Verse 20.

"It is no use walking anywhere to preach unless we preach as we walk."

ST. FRANCIS OF ASSISI
(1182-1226)

THE *Sawdust Trail*

Chapter One

FROM THE
PARSONAGE AND
THE INN

John Wesley
(1703-1791)

George Whitefield
(1714-1770)

"Wanted a curacy in a good sporting country where the duty is light and the neighborhood convivial."

So ran an advertisement in an eighteenth-century English newspaper. Never had the established church of the realm sunk so low in decadence and laxity. Dr. Samuel Johnson maintained that "no man can now be a bishop for his learning and piety. His only chance of promotion is his being connected with some one who has parliamentary interest."

Eighteenth-century archbishops and bishops behaved like mighty potentates. One of them, Bishop Hurd (1720-1808), commonly called "The Beauty of Holiness," rode in a coach complete with liveried lackeys to his cathedral just a quarter of a mile away. In 1776 he had been Preceptor to the Prince of Wales.

Lambeth Palace became a place of roistering and notoriety during the time that Archbishop Frederick Cornwallis (1713-1783) occupied its time-honored walls. The godly Selina, Countess of Huntington, a rarity among the upper classes, protested loudly to King George III and his consort, Queen Caroline. Upon hearing from so impeccable a source of the feastings and partyings, the King angrily told the Primate of the "grief and concern with which my breast was affected."

Howbeit, the kings and queens were not much better. George I imprisoned his wife, Sofia Dorothea of Zell, in the castel of Ahlden, thirty miles from Hanover, in order to live openly with an assortment of mistresses. The Georgian gentry sat in curtained box pews where they could sleep or flirt free from disturbance, while the working man was relegated to rough benches at the back of the church.

In the early years of the seventeenth century gin caused the downfall of both men and women. Good morals were despised; even the poor could get drunk for a penny. In London they had seventeen thousand gin shops from which to choose!

George II was described as having "united the morals of a rake with the tastes of a boor." Never did a country have a greater need of a religious awakening than England.

Finally it came from the mouth of John Wesley, who bluntly declared that "nine tenths of the men in England have no more religion than horses." Of the clergy he said, "These are the pests of the Christian world, the grand nuisance of mankind, a stink in the nostrils of God."

John Benjamin Wesley, a descendant of Adam Loftus, primate of Ireland, was the fifteenth child and second surviving son of the Reverend Samuel Wesley and Susanna, his wife.

From the age of five, young John was taught by his mother—to all accounts a most exacting teacher, for she allowed him only one day in which to learn the entire alphabet. Even as a child, John Wesley had firmness of character. His father maintained that "our Jack" would do nothing "unless he could give a reason for it."

He was only eight years old when admitted to the communion. On June 24, 1720, he was elected a scholar of Christ Church, Oxford. On July 18 he matriculated, his age then being given as sixteen.

In one letter his mother gave explicit approval of his intention to study for Holy Orders, although she confessed, "your father and I seldom think alike."

On September 19, 1725, Wesley became a deacon, and the following March was elected a fellow of Lincoln College. In the fall of 1728 he was ordained a priest, taking to heart the words of Thomas Haywood that when a man entered the priesthood he was "bidding defiance to all mankind." In Wesley's case they were prophetic.

The following year, returning to Oxford, John found his brother Charles closely associated with two fellow-undergraduates, William Morgan, an Irishman, and Robert Kirkham. Because of their strict religious convictions, in-

cluding the practice of weekly communion and particular
rules for study, the group members were familiarly called
"Methodists." Upon joining them, John Wesley soon became their leader. Students dubbed him "Curator of the
Holy Club."

Rules of discipline included such practical acts as helping
the poor, clothing school children and visiting prisoners
in the castle, to whom they read prayers twice a week, but
the Methodists were far from morbid, allowing several
forms of recreation.

Rising at four in the morning to cure himself of lying
awake at night, John was ready to pray for an hour at five.
Each evening, also at five, he spent an hour of prayer.
Everything personal had to work like clockwork.

Precise about everything, he was no ascetic, but strict
discipline failed to curb his individuality. He enjoyed playing cards. Meeting his fellow men daily in the streets improved his understanding of human nature, an advantage he
would later appreciate when preaching to crowds. One
day a week only was put aside for friendly correspondence.
Wesley kept a lively diary and accurate personal accounts.
In 1733 he published a collection of daily prayers for the
use of his students.

On June 11, 1734, John Wesley preached before the
University what his brother Charles called "his Jacobite
sermon." First, however, he tactfully submitted it to the
vice-chancellor for approval.

John Wesley's interest in the opposite sex blossomed
when he met Mary Granville Pendarves (more often
known as Mary Delany). In their correspondence Wesley
was "Cyrus" to Mary's "Aspasia." There was a warm,
genuine interest on both sides.

In 1734 the Reverend Samuel Wesley was anxious to see

John appointed his successor at Epworth. When another son, Samuel, refused the post, the father angrily exhorted John to follow in his footsteps. John refused, declaring he thought he could do more good by remaining at Oxford. However, in a letter dated April 15, 1735, just prior to his father's death on April 25, John seemingly changed his mind, only to lose the opportunity when Edmund Gibson, then Bishop of London, opposed his promotion.

On September 18, John joined the Georgia mission, promoted by John Burton, the mission trustee. Most of the trustees were Dissenters.

Burton introduced Wesley to General James Edward Oglethorpe, who had once been aide-de-camp to Prince Eugene of Savoy, had served in parliament for thirty-two years, and in 1733 had founded Savannah, Georgia.

With his brother Charles and several others, Wesley sailed aboard the *Simmonds* from Gravesend on October 14, 1735. For some reason the boat was detained at Cowes until December 10. The Methodists' fellow travelers were twenty-six German Moravians, under the guidance of David Nitschmann (1696-1772), their newly-appointed bishop, and John lost no time in learning to speak German. He already knew French, which he declared to be "the poorest, meanest language in Europe." (Later, in 1737, for the purpose of speaking to Jewish emigrants in Georgia, he successfully mastered Spanish.)

On February 6, the *Simmonds* reached Savannah. The following day General Oglethorpe introduced John to August Gottlieb Spangenberg, later a bishop, (1704-1792), whose subsequent discussions convinced Wesley of the importance of evangelism. Staying a month with Spangenberg, Wesley met and liked many of his colleagues. On February

28 he attended the ordination of Anton Seiffart as Moravian bishop of Georgia, a ceremony which he praised for its "simplicity, as well as solemnity."

Wesley's prime object in going to Georgia was to serve as a missionary to the Indians. In Savannah he daily preached and read the liturgy, traveling through swamps and across rivers to reach out-of-the way settlements, and often sleeping on the open ground. As firm a believer in fasting as he still was in dieting, he also walked barefoot among the children "to encourage those who had no shoes."

At first his preaching was successful, but his rigorous discipline soon became distasteful to settlers and Indians alike. His sermons were considered too personal, together with his punctilious insistence upon such fine points as the immersion of infants at baptism and use of the mixed chalice, upsetting to many people. Neither did they approve of his holding the morning service at five, and the communion-office with sermon at eleven. His introduction of new hymns was similarly unpopular, as was his strict ruling regarding the suitability of individual communicants. It is interesting to note that Wesley excluded "dissenters as unbaptized." When he held private religious "society" meetings, the settlers cried, "We are protestants."

Finally, becoming the subject of enmity and persecution through his attempts to influence the secular affairs of the colony, he relinquished his work.

Embarking on December 22, 1737, from Charleston (then Charlestown) South Carolina, where his first hymn book had recently been published, Wesley landed the following February at Deal, England, to find that his colleague George Whitefield was about to set out for Georgia. Wesley was opposed to his going and wrote telling him so, yet avoided seeing his old friend.

Meeting Peter Buhler, who was newly arrived from Germany, Wesley took him on a visit to Oxford. Buhler founded a "religious society" at Fetter Lane Chapel, which Wesley joined; and although he continued to officiate in Anglican churches using the rites as established in the Book of Common Prayer, at the meetings of Buhler's society he prayed extemporaneously.

Wesley had the experience of "conversion" at a society meeting in Aldersgate, his brother Charles having been "converted" first. Writing to his brother Samuel, John said he believed that this new experience was but a step along the way.

Because of his admiration for the Moravians, Wesley visited Holland and North Germany. At Marienborn he called on Count Nicholas Lewis Zinzendorf (1700-1760) who soon set him to work digging in his garden. Zinzendorf went to New York in 1741, visited the Moravian colony in Pennsylvania, and founded a settlement at Bethlehem. Back in London, John called on Edmund Gibson, Bishop of London, in company with Charles Wesley. Asking the Bishop to determine whether "religious societies" were "conventicles," Gibson replied that he thought not, although he was careful to add, "I determine nothing."

During a month spent at Oxford toward the end of 1738, Wesley drew up rules for the Moravian societies.

Because Wesley was a late joiner of the Holy Club, George Whitefield's type of open-air preaching had at first not appealed to his sense of "decency and order." He changed his mind after describing at Bristol the Sermon on the Mount, which he maintained was a "pretty remarkable precedent of field-preaching, though I suppose there were churches at that time also." The next day, Monday, April 2, 1739, Wesley spoke "from a little eminence in a ground adjoining to the city, to about three thousand people."

On May 12 he was at the Horsefair, Bristol, laying the foundation stone of "a room" later called "the New Room," sometimes called the first Methodist Chapel. At Bath on June 5, he encountered the notorious dandy, "Beau" (Richard) Nash, who tried to prevent his preaching to a great crowd.

Wearing an effeminate white hat, Nash swaggered before the company of ordinary men and women, a peacock among dowdy sparrows. However, Nash had better have stayed home, for Wesley's gift of repartee left him at a disadvantage.

After telling Wesley that he spoke illegally, Nash commented, "Besides, your preaching frightens people out of their wits."

"Sir," replied Wesley with a wry smile, "did you ever hear me preach?"

"No," replied the "Beau."

"How, then, can you judge of what you never heard?"

"I judge by common report," countered the dandy.

"Common report is not enough," replied Wesley icily. "Give me leave, sir, to ask, is not your name Nash?"

"It is," was the answer.

"Sir," snapped Wesley, "*I dare not judge of you by common report.*"

From this humble beginning, Wesley said,

> We went forth to seek that which was lost, more eminently lost, to call the most flagrant, hardened, desperate sinners to repentance. To this end we preached in the Horsefair at Bristol, in Kingswood, in Newcastle, among the colliers in Staffordshire and the tinners in

Cornwell, in Southwark, Wapping, Moorfields, Drury Lane, at London. Did any man ever pick out such places as these in order to find serious, regular, well-disposed people? How many such might there be in any of them I know not. But this I know, that four in five of those who are now with us were not of that number but were wallowing in their blood, till God by us said unto them "Live."

Wesley shook off earlier associations with his Moravian and Calvinistic friends to organize his own Methodist movement. Then, turning to "the byways and hedges" with his brother Charles, he "began those tireless missionary journeys over the land by which, in the words of Benjamin Terry's *A History of England for Schools*, they stirred England as she had not been stirred since the early days of the Reformation."

Born of the Industrial Revolution, Methodism as preached by John Wesley was primarily a religion for the poor, for he made them feel important, like the rich, with souls equally worthy of salvation. "Liberty, equality and fraternity" were taught by Wesley years before the French Revolution. The poor were amazed to find a man speaking in a cultured Oxford voice who was actually interested in whether they even had a soul!

Among the first to accept his Methodist teachings were the miners, then a tough, brutal and dissolute segment of mankind. To these men he brought the comforts of both the Bible and his own hymn book.

Wesley, often called the Father of Modern Evangelism, himself sums up the form of evangelism he so firmly advocated in his own words:

This love, we believe to be the medicine of life, the never-failing remedy for all the evils of a disordered world, for all the miseries and vices of men. Wherever this is, there are virtue and happiness going hand in hand. There is humbleness of mind, gentleness, long suffering, the whole image of God, and at the same time a peace that passeth all understanding and joy unspeakable and full of glory.

This religion we long to see established in the world, a religion of love, and joy, and peace, having its seat in the inmost soul, but ever showing itself by its fruits continually springing forth, not only in all innocence (for love worketh no ill to his neighbor) but likewise in every kind of beneficence, spreading virtue and happiness all around it.

The plain religion now propagated is Love. And can you oppose this without being an enemy to mankind?

Owners of ale-houses and places of ill-repute, robbed of customers who were finding new meaning to life in Wesley's popular teachings, were violent in their persecution of him and his wandering preachers. Spurred on by country squires, who in many cases controlled their church endowments, Wesley's fellow Anglican clergy were little better. Often the behavior of attacking mobs could be traced directly to these so-called "men of God." One curate, the Reverend George White of Colne, Lancashire, who later died from alcohol poisoning, promised that "each man shall receive a pint of ale in advance, and other proper encouragements" to break up the Methodist meeting.

Wesley on this occasion was met by a raging mob:

> . . . A drunken rabble came with clubs and staves in a tumultuous and riotous manner . . . I had scarcely gone ten yards when a man . . . struck me with his fist in the face with all his might. Quickly after, another threw his

stick at my head. Another man, cursing and swearing in the most shocking manner, cried out, "Bring him away."

On another occasion a clergyman accompanied by several "gentlemen" came equipped with huntsmen and hounds to beleaguer him, "but the dogs were wiser than the men, for they could not bring them to make any noise at all."

In the face of such physical hazards, Wesley showed amazing courage, even making a point of studying mob psychology. Often this resulted in earning the respect of those very men who had been sent to destroy him.

Once an ox was actually chased by a mob into Wesley's praying congregation. Frightened by the screams of the faithful, the unfortunate animal "ran around and round one way and the other, and at length broke through the midst of them clear away, leaving us calmly rejoicing and praising God."

Even this was mild compared with the incident of the bull. At Pensford, a poor creature that had been baited was actually driven, torn and bleeding, against the very table which Wesley was using as an improvised pulpit. Wesley graphically records the scene: "They strove several times to throw it down by thrusting the helpless beast against it, who of himself stirred no more than a log of wood. I once or twice put aside his head with my hand that the blood might not drop upon my clothes."

For three decades John Wesley was to know such treatment. When struck by a stone he would wipe the blood from his face and continue preaching. Church bells were rung to drown his voice, he was pelted with stink-bombs, and on one occasion a man was even bribed to shout, "Fresh salmon!" as a tasteful temptation for the congregation to desert him.

At Epworth, however, where John Romley, the curate to whom Wesely's father had shown much kindness, had treated the son discourteously, no mob could be roused to annoy the wandering preacher. Wesley writes, "Accordingly, at six I came and found such a congregation as I believe Epworth never saw before. I stood near the east end of the church upon my father's tombstone, and cried, 'The Kingdom of Heaven is not meat and drink, but righteousness, and peace, and joy in the Holy Ghost.' "

There is now a tradition that Wesley's footprints are imbedded in "sections of two ferruginous concretions in the slab" of his father's tombstone.

In time Wesley opened various chapels, where men and women sat apart. In 1743 he published "Thoughts of Marriage and Celibacy," in which he stated that he preferred the latter. Perhaps this led indirectly to the breaking up of his romance with Grace Murray, who was in charge of his orphan house at Newcastle-on-Tyne. It was there that Grace was to nurse him when he was ill in 1748.

A daughter of poor parents, Grace was the widow of Alexander Murray, a sailor who had been drowned at sea. Although Wesley proposed marriage to her, he seems to have postponed the ceremony. Then Grace met John Bennet, one of Wesley's own preachers, and—no doubt having grown weary of waiting—married him, instead. Wesley was deeply hurt.

Persuaded by well-meaning friends that he should marry, he chose Mary Vazeille, a former domestic servant who was seven years his junior. She had made a "good" marriage with one Anthony Vazeille, who at the time of his death in 1747 had bequeathed to her a fortune of three thousand pounds.

Mary had four children, Noah, the youngest, being

under five years of age. In a surprising marriage settlement for those days when women had few legal rights of their own, her personal property was secured to her own exclusive use. Although Wesley had sprained his ankle so that he was forced to "preach on his knees," he was well enough to accompany Mrs. Vazeille to the altar. His brother Charles seems to have been one of the last to hear of his unhappy marriage.

The union began well enough, Mrs. Wesley being described as "well qualified" for her eminent position as wife of the Methodist leader. She did not persuade him to curtail any of his strenuous labors, and accompanied him on his second visit to Scotland in 1753. However, she was short-tempered, and deeply resented Wesley's corresponding with female Methodists, however innocent the motive. To observers it seemed that John and Mary Wesley could not live with—or without—each other! Even after she left him to live with her married daughter in 1771 she was back again the following year to help with his missionary work. In 1776 she left him for good, yet in her will, dated September 4, 1779, she bequeathed to him a "mourning gold ring, in token that I die in love and friendship towards him."

Wesley had even made Mary his residuary legatee, referring to the children of her married daughter as "my dear granddaughters." By a twist of fate, the widened roadway adjoining the churchyard of St. Giles, Camberwell, now passes over Mary Wesley's grave.

Following his marriage, Wesley resigned his fellowship at Oxford. From his Methodist society he never received more than thirty pounds a year, although it did allow him some traveling expenses. His publications and tracts made him rich, although the proceeds of these he gave away, sometimes to the amount of a thousand pounds a year. Describing his plate to the Commissioners of Excise in 1776, Wesley recorded "two silver teaspoons at London, and two at Bristol" as the grand total. When he believed himself near death in 1753, he calmly composed his own epitaph, and then made sure of his not leaving, after his debts were paid, ten pounds behind him.

His missionary travels read like a guidebook, the British Isles serving as his parish. After 1747 he crossed the choppy Irish Sea forty-seven times. He considered his missionary tour of Holland, made when he was eighty, to be more of a vacation than anything else.

Upon one occasion Wesley preached beneath the wych-elm at Bishop Burton, near Beverley, an event which was annually commemorated by his followers until 1836 when, during a storm, the great tree crashed to the ground. Undaunted, the Methodists employed a local sculptor to carve a bust of Wesley from the trunk. This was placed in their chapel close by, where it stood for sixty years until, having been attacked by woodworm, it was thrown out.

Fortunately, the vicar of the local Anglican church noticed the discarded figurehead lying on the ground. Thinking it would look well in his own edifice, he purchased it for only two pounds, and scolded the Methodists from his own pulpit for having "sold their master for forty pieces of silver." A local craftsman was called in to treat the bust with paraffin oil. His bill read,

> To re-baptizing John Wesley, and curing him of the worms—25s.

During Wesley's travels, preaching laymen took charge of the society work. They were each assigned circuits, and formed the first annual conference on June 25, 1744.

Among Wesley's many writings was, surprisingly, a treatise on medicine entitled "Primitive Physic," published in 1747, which ran into twenty editions. Among the "medicines" he prescribed were cobwebs, groundsel, onions and frankincense.

John Wesley preached with the insight of a statesman, believing that the ground he had won could be retained only by organization. In 1791, at the time of his death, there were more than a hundred thousand Methodists. He had no wish to break from the established Church of England, but soon after his death the Methodist body withdrew entirely.

In America, where Wesley himself had not been especially successful, the Methodist movement fell on rich ground, while in England it influenced people of all walks of life, even some Anglican clergymen. The fox hunting vicar and absentee incumbent in time gave way to men like Toplady, author of "Rock of Ages." A spirit of philanthropy spread through English society. Literature ceased to be obscene; the upper classes strove to repair the open profligacy that had so long disgraced them. As America's President Woodrow Wilson noted many years afterwards, "The Church was dead and Wesley awakened it; the poor were neglected and Wesley sought them out; the gospel was shrunken into formulas and Wesley flung it fresh upon the air once more in the speech of common men."

In contrast to Wesley, who was born in a parsonage, his greatest contemporary evangelist, George Whitefield, was born in an inn. No introvert, from a young man he was convinced he had been chosen to be God's Mouthpiece, and by the time he was twenty-six years old he had preached to crowds estimated at 80,000. His popularity was unrivaled.

Frankly, he says, "The Circumstance of my being born in an Inn, has often been of Service to me in exciting my Endeavours to make good my Mother's Expectations, and so follow the Example of my dear Saviour, who was born in a Manger belonging to an Inn."

His parents were Thomas and Elizabeth Whitefield, proprietors of the Bell Inn, Southgate Street, Gloucester. Although an inn might not have been an ideal place to raise a child (the eighteenth century writer Thomas Brown had described such a place as "a little Sodom, where as many Vices are daily practised as ever were known"), George does not seem to have suffered unduly. His own description of youthful depravity appears overcolored, being little different from that experienced by the average boy of his generation. Although he was impetuous and emotional, his favorite game was playing at being a minister.

The young George Whitefield was a frustrated actor who was very fond of reading plays and often played truant from school to do so. One day, while reading aloud a play to his sister, he made the somewhat startling announcement, "God intends something for me which we know not of."

Re-entering the Grammar School for a short sojourn, he was persuaded by his mother to apply for a servitor's admission to Pembroke College, Oxford. She had been told how a young man might work his way through college.

With his tavern training, George Whitefield's early days as a servitor at Pembroke College were highly successful. His services were much sought by fortunate young gentlemen of means who could afford them.

Being a servitor, George Whitefield had no lectures to pay for. Complaining of "young Students spending their Substance in extravagant living," he refused to "join in

John Wesley at 67—a 1770 print from an original painting by N. Hone.

George Whitefield (1714-1770). His field preaching had a powerful appeal for Colonial America.

John Lewis Dyer preaching from a Rocky Mountain bar. He always traveled the roads unarmed.

"Father" Dyer, the "Snowshoe Itinerant." He walked forty miles each Sunday, serving three congregations.

His mother was buried in the dead of night because she was "only a gypsy," but staid Boston hailed Rodney Smith as "a spiritual phenomenon, an intellectual prodigy and a musical and oratorical phenomenon."

D. L. Moody in a characteristic pose. Personal magnetism and a gift for interpreting the Bible overcame grammatical lapses.

PHOTOGRAPH BY WINFRED E. CHAPIN

Billy Sunday displays one of his famous preaching stances on the steps of the White House.

General Evangeline Booth. She knew what it was to be a flower girl and a match seller, and successfully defended her street-corner musicians in court.

"Sweet Daddy" Grace had 3,000,000 followers in more than 60 cities.

"Sister"—Aimee Semple McPherson—in Egypt in 1930.

Woodmont, the "Mountain of
the House of the Lord," home
of Father and Mother Divine.

Rheba Crawford, called by Walter Winchell "the Angel of Broadway." Notorious characters of New York's underworld were among her staunchest defenders.

Billy Graham with the late President Kennedy.

their Excess," being called "a singular, odd fellow" and left to his own devices.

Convinced that God had singled him out for some extraordinary purpose, George Whitefield struggled to discover what it was.

The opportunity to join the Holy Club finally arose when Charles Wesley, a tutor at Christ Church, invited him to breakfast. Eventually he was introduced to John and other Methodists at the university, following their example of living by a set rule, taking the sacrament on Sundays, fasting twice a week and ministering to the needy. The "gentlemen" he had attended as servitor now ignored him altogether because of his new connection.

The Wesleys' methodical regimentation, followed by Whitefield's own adventure into asceticism when he wore "woolen Gloves, a patched Gown, and dirty shoes," brought little peace of mind. He tried so hard to please God that his fanatical zeal resulted in his doctor's ordering a long rest. It was during this period of ill-health that George Whitefield experienced what he called a "new birth," when his body seemed filled with "a sense of the pardoning love of God and oneness with Him. Thus," he says, "were the Days of my Mourning ended."

Home to Gloucester went Whitefield, but not to carry out his doctor's prescription of rest. His ministry to "tell men the truth" had to begin at once; there could be no delay. God had spoken and George Whitefield was his prophet!

Forming a small society, which seems to have been the pattern for every new preacher, he remarked that it "had quickly the Honour of being despised at Gloucester." He visited the sick and preached in the jail, where conditions were so filthy that it was hard to find a regular chaplain with enough Christian charity to minister to the prisoners. Whitefield's dynamic career of service had begun.

When well-meaning friends suggested he should enter the ministry, he hesitated. One day, when he was leaving Gloucester Cathedral, he was told by a verger that Martin Benson, Bishop of Gloucester, wished to see him. Without his knowledge, Whitefield had been recommended by Lady Selwyn to the Bishop for ordination. So impressed was the Bishop with the interview that he dramatically announced, "Notwithstanding I have declared I would not ordain anyone under three and twenty, yet I shall think it is my duty to ordain you whenever you come for holy orders."

The practical Bishop then presented the young man with five golden guineas. On Sunday, June 20, 1736, George Whitefield, aged twenty-one, was admitted to Deacon's orders in Gloucester's historic cathedral.

Conscious of his youth, Whitefield prepared for the occasion by rising early and praying over St. Paul's Epistle to Timothy ". . . more particularly over that Precept, 'Let *no* man despise thy Youth.' " During the service he was quite composed and could "think of nothing but Samuel's standing a little Child before the Lord."

Shortly after his ordination, Whitefield had the degree of Bachelor of Arts conferred upon him at Oxford.

The following Sunday, in the Church of St. Mary de Crypt, he preached his first sermon, bravely criticizing the fashionable social gatherings known as "assemblies." A large congregation attended to hear the "boy parson"— many, Whitefield admits, out of curiosity. On this occasion he was described as being "graceful, and well proportioned; his stature rather above middle size. His complexion was very fair. His eyes were of a dark blue colour, and small, but sprightly. He had a squint in one of them, occasioned either by ignorance, or the carelessness of the nurse who attended him in the measles when he was about four years old."

His first sermon was said to have driven five members of the congregation "mad" when he criticized them for "revellings . . . chambering and wantonness." Complaints were made to Bishop Benson, who ruefully remarked that he hoped the "madness might not be forgotten before next Sunday."

John Wesley had sent Whitefield an appeal to come to America and help with the missionary work, but twelve months were to elapse before he could leave. In the meantime, the boy preacher achieved a phenomenal popularity. Thousands flocked to hear him in London, Gloucester, Bristol, and even fashionable Bath. He collected great a- mounts of money for the Georgia mission and charity schools, upsetting the regular incumbents of those churches in which he was guest preacher. They were quick to dub him a "spiritual pickpocket."

His popularity with the masses brought mumblings of discord from other sources, particularly a leading Church of England newspaper, *The Weekly Miscellany*. His un- orthodox habit of mixing freely with Dissenters displeased this auspicious organ, Whitefield wrote, "A report was spread abroad, that the Bishop of London, upon the com- plaint of the clergy, intended to silence me. . . ."

When he preached his farewell sermon before departing for Georgia, the behavior of the crowds was amazing. He says, "I was nearly half-an-hour going out to the door. All ranks gave vent to their passions. Thousands and thou- sands of prayers were put up for me. They would run and stop me in the alleys, hug me in their arms, and follow me with wishful looks."

On December 30, hard-pressed by his weeping followers, he boarded the troopship *Whitaker*, which for some reason did not finally leave England until February 2, 1738. That date was an important one in the history of American evangelism. George Whitefield was on the way.

While the *Whitaker* was still anchored at Deal, John Wesley (his brother Charles having already returned) disembarked from another ship, thoroughly disheartened by his personal experiences in the New World. Even when Wesley saw fit to write Whitefield a letter completely at variance with the one urging him to go to Georgia, the boy preacher refused to alter his plans. In this important matter he now had to follow the dictates of his own conscience, even though it meant ignoring the advice of his good friend and former idol. Reprovingly, he wrote Wesley that "It is not fit the colony should be left without a shepherd."

Once at sea, Whitefield lost no time in ministering to his fellow passengers of all ages. His methods were sometimes somewhat drastic, as in the case of the little boy not more than four years of age who refused to say his prayers.

> I bid the Child kneel down before me, but he would not, till I took hold of its two feet, and forced it down. I then bid it say the Lord's Prayer, (being informed by his Mother he could say it if he would) but he obstinately refused, till at last after I had given it several Blows, it said its Prayers as well as could be expected, and I gave it some figs for a Reward.

Landing at Savannah, May 7, 1738, Whitefield proved a success from the beginning. In spite of an attack of fever, he began to preach at once, visiting outlying villages as well as prominent residents. He accomplished in four months as much as most men would have done in four years. Even the "many loose Livers" in the colony were charmed by the earnestness of his sermons. His own burning passion made the dullest passages of scripture come vividly alive. Unable to make verbal contact with Tomo Chichi, the Indian chief who, like Pocahontas before him, had been presented at England's royal court, Whitefield simply pointed to the fire and warned him of Hell.

Unlike Wesley, Whitefield did not annoy the colonists by enforcing rigid church discipline. Yet religion he preached wherever he went. If he tipped a retainer he gave the man a tract as well. Whitefield's doctrine of repentance and new birth attracted all classes, including dissenters. He believed that he knew God, and in this personal conviction dwelt his strength of appeal.

Deciding that the settlement was in dire need of an orphanage, he vowed to establish one, an idea first suggested to him by Charles Wesley. First, however, he needed money. Also, he had not yet been ordained a priest. When George Whitefield sailed back to England from Charlestown on September 9, these necessities, plus his determination to "hasten back as soon as possible," were uppermost in his mind. He little guessed how stormy would be the months before he could again set out for America.

The voyage home was a hard one. The provisions ran short, and water was rationed to a pint a day, and "no one knows where we are," he wrote in his *Journal*, "but God does, and that is sufficient."

Safely landed in England at last, Whitefield found to his embarrassment that his own *Journal* covering the outbound voyage to America had been published privately. Unfortunately, the outspoken language offended many

readers, so that the "boy preacher" found his former popularity waning. He was criticized upon every side. Two
days in London were enough for him to "confide" to his
current *Journal* the disturbing fact that five churches had
even closed their pulpits to him, while many clergymen
thought he should be banished from the realm.

However, Bishop Benson, still his friend, ordained him a
priest at Oxford on January 14. Whitefield, to whom
preaching was both meat and drink, rejoiced that in the
first sermon delivered in his new state, his voice behaved
like a "trumpet."

Closed churches proved no deterrent to the eager new
priest. Gathering together vast crowds in the open, he not
only converted them to his way of thinking but took
collections toward building his orphanage. Selina, Countess
of Huntingdon, was his most ardent supporter. To one of
his sermons she inveigled not only Horace Walpole and the
Duchess of Marlborough, but also none other than Lady
Suffolk, mistress to King George II himself.

Bishop Benson saw fit to write Lady Selina an account
of her protégé's ordination with the fervent hope that she
would no longer find fault with him (the bishop). "Though
mistaken on some points," he told her, "I think him a very
pious, well-meaning young man, with good abilities and
great zeal. I find his Grace of Canterbury thinks highly
of him."

On February 17, 1739, Whitefield delivered his first outdoor sermon to colliers on Kingswood Hill, near Bristol.
These unfortunate men were most unpopular in the city,
and shopkeepers barred their doors to them whenever they
were in the vicinity. Of this notable occasion Whitefield
wrote, "After Dinner, therefore, I went upon a Mount,
and spoke to as many People as came upon me. They were

upwards of two Hundred. Blessed be God, I have now broke the Ice; I believe I never was more acceptable to my Master than when I was standing to teach those Hearers in the open Fields."

The miners were so touched by his message of new birth that there were "white gutters made by their tears, (which) plentifully fell down their black cheeks, as they came out of their coal pits."

Whitefield had inaugurated preaching in the fields; nothing now stood in his way. According to his own journals, "so great a multitude of coaches, foot and horsemen," came to hear him preach on Rose Green Common "that they covered three acres and were computed at twenty thousand people."

Meanwhile in London only one church remained open to the preaching phenomenon, and this not for long. Whitefield was obliged to "repeat that mad Trick" of preaching out of doors, this time in Moorfields, then an elm-landscaped resort. Whitefield often preached so early in the morning that it was necessary for the congregation to arrive clutching their lanterns.

Some of the converts were not always appreciated. Joseph Periam "prayed so as to be heard four Story high" and was committed by his long-suffering neighbors to Bethlehem Hospital.

While Whitefield awaited his passage back to America, having been appointed minister of Savannah by the Georgia Trustees, "the Hosts of Midian" raged around him. The *Weekly Miscellany* declared Whitefield "a raw novice" and said that he fancied himself an apostle, setting himself up as a teacher not only of the laity but of "the learned clergy . . . *many of them learned before he was born.*" Even Dr. Philip Doddridge, speaking for leading Dissenters, said disapprovingly that "supposing him sincere and in good earnest, "I still fancy that he is but a weak man—much too positive, says rash things, and is bold and enthusiastic . . . I think what Mr. Whitefield [*sic*] says and does comes but little short of an assumption of inspiration or infallibility."

Nevertheless, in spite of such unfavorable outbursts, when on August 14, 1739, Whitefield again embarked for America on the *Elizabeth*, he left behind hundreds of converted followers who failed to see why he had to go "in search of Indians" when his outdoor congregations in England were limitless.

The unfortunate Periam, released from the madhouse, accompanied Whitefield by order of the authorities. Declared Whitefield as a parting barb to his enemies, "My Master makes me more than a conqueror."

He could well crow. In his pockets were approximately a thousand pounds for the erection of his beloved orphanage, while the colony trustees had promised him a grant of five hundred acres upon which to build it.

Arriving October 30, he proceeded to Philadelphia, preaching from the Court House Gallery, where six thousand people jammed the street below to hear him. According to the *Pennsylvania Gazette*, they "stood in awful silence." Benjamin Franklin noted with amazement the effect of Whitefield's delivery, writing, "It is wonderful to see the change soon made in the manners of our inhabitants . . . The Multitudes of all sects and denominations that attended his sermons were enormous." Franklin advertised in the *Pennsylvania Gazette* his intention to publish two volumes of Whitefield sermons and two of the *Journals*.

En route to New York he met and preached with the Presbyterian evangelist Gilbert Tennent, known as the "Son of Thunder." Whitefield called him a man who "went to the Bottom indeed, and did not daub with untempered Mortar." Tennent was also an exponent of outdoor preaching, where he was accused of allowing his congregation to stand "in the snow night and day for the benefit of his beastly braying."

Whitefield was glad to turn his horse south after finding the New York churches closed against him. In Maryland, Virginia and the Carolinas great throngs of people turned out to listen. The women of Maryland rather displeased him, being "enslaved" like the menfolk to such diversions as "their Bottle and their Hounds." In Virginia he was invited to dine with the Governor, preaching at Williamsburg to a "numerous Congregation." He complained of the lack of "any true vital Piety" in Virginia. In North Carolina he was fascinated by the wolves that howled nightly "like a Kennel of Hounds."

South Carolina really shocked him, as he did not approve of the country dancing, and especially of a woman he saw "dancing a Jigg." He informed her "how well pleased the Devil was at every Step she took." The ministers of religion he considered little better, complaining, "I hear of no stirring among the dry Bones."

George Whitefield was thankful to be back at last in Savannah, where upon arriving January 10, 1740, he immediately began to plan the orphanage. At this time the *Virginia Gazette* published a poem in his honor:

> See! See! He comes, the heav'nly Sound
> Flows from his charming Tongue;
> Rebellious Men are seiz'd with Fear,
> With deep Conviction stung.

When Selina, Countess of Huntingdon, read the verse back in England, she was pleased indeed.

The site chosen by Whitefield for his orphanage was ten miles out of the city "because [there] the Children will be more free from bad Examples." He named it Bethesda. The two-story building was to have a "hip roof" and 60 by 40 feet dimensions.

While the building was under way Whitefield hired a house in Savannah for the orphans already under his care, leaving them in the care of friends who had sailed with him upon the *Elizabeth* from England. His zeal to provide homes for orphans already installed in happy surroundings soon provoked trouble. Whitefield called the American clergy "slothful Shepherds" and "Dumb Dogs," and when he visited Charleston the Reverend Alexander Garden retaliated by preaching a sermon entitled, "Those who have turned the world upside down have come hither also." Whitefield was not disturbed. In his reply he used the appropriate text: "Alexander the coopersmith hath done me much evil; the Lord reward him according to his works."

With William Seward, also recently arrived from England, Whitefield set out April 2 in the sloop *Savannah* for Newcastle, Pennsylvania, where they landed ten days later. On the way, deciding that he should marry "a daughter of Abraham," Whitefield penned one of the most preposterous proposals of matrimony ever written. The recipient was a certain "Miss E.," Elizabeth Delamotte, daughter of a magistrate at Blendon, Middlesex, England. In it he said:

> I make no great profession to you, because I believe you think me sincere. The passionate expressions which carnal courtiers use, I think, ought to be avoided by those that would marry in the Lord. I can only promise, by the help of God, "to keep my matrimonial vow, and to do what I

can towards helping you forward in the great work of your salvation."

"Miss E." was not impressed; she promptly refused him.

News of Whitefield's arrival at Newcastle quickly spread over the surrounding countryside, and thousands of people flocked to hear him. The American colonies were now experiencing a spontaneous spiritual awakening with Whitefield as pilot. His energy was unbounding. The inhabitants of New York, Long Island, and finally his favorite Philadelphia, rallied to seek salvation. On Society Hill in the latter place a platform was erected from which he preached to thousands. So impressed was Benjamin Franklin that when Whitefield appealed for funds to supply Bethesda, he emptied his pockets.

Philadelphia's young ladies at a special meeting were so entranced with Whitefield's "musical voice" that "their cries might be heard a great Way off." One remained so distraught that "at midnight," Whitefield records, "I was desired to come to one who was in strong Agonies."

Back in Savannah by June 5, he was glad to find that his own parishioners were so aware of their sinfulness even "the little Lambs" cried bitterly. After services the people would follow him home through the streets, singing and praying aloud. Religious fervor ran high.

Later that month, Whitefield journeyed to Charlestown where Commissary Garden had summoned him to appear before an ecclesiastical court, reputed to be the first ever convened in the colonies. He was required to answer questions concerning irregularities in his doctrine and practices. "Then he [the Commissary of Charlestown]" records Whitefield, "charged me with Enthusiasm and Pride, for speaking against the generality of the Clergy." He boldly defined the court as a prejudiced body, appealing to the High Court of Chancery, which delayed the Charlestown hearing for a year and a day.

Such a charge might have disturbed some men, but not George Whitefield, who immediately set out to save New England. Landing at Newport, Rhode Island, he lost little time in going to Boston where, it is interesting to note, the Church of England ministers were more friendly than the dissenting ones. He even preached on Boston Common, the inhabitants thrilling to the sound of his "trumpeting" voice.

Yet, unlike Wesley, Whitefield was not an intellectual. He deliberately set himself apart from the views of organized study.

In spite of the fact that he saw fit to criticize the staid Bostonians for their funeral custom of keeping silent at the graveside, they generously forgave him, mustering a record gathering estimated at 30,000 people to bid him farewell. Whitefield, accustomed to vast crowds, had never seen anything like this in all the colonies. Even Governor Jonathan Belcher was on hand to take Whitefield to the ferry in his own coach.

An important event during the Massachusetts revival was Whitefield's meeting with Jonathan Edwards, famed divine, of whom he wrote, "I have not seen his Fellow in all New England." So impressed was Whitefield with Mrs. Edwards that he was moved to "renew those Prayers" that he might find a wife of his own.

Visiting both Harvard and Yale, he preached to the latter's students upon the ill effects of an unconverted ministry. He was not especially impressed with what he found, confiding to his *Journal* that "as for the Universities, I believe, it may be said, their Light is become Darkness,

Darkness that may be felt, and is complained of by the most godly Ministers."

In Philadelphia on November 9 he was delighted to find that his friends had built a new tabernacle for him. In fact, "any preacher of any religious persuasion . . . even if the Mufti of Constantinople were to send a missionary to preach Mohammedanism," would be welcome to use its pulpit. The tabernacle, known as the New Building, had been erected close to the corner of Mulberry and Fourth Streets. Today it is remembered as the original site of the University of Pennsylvania, on whose present campus Whitefield's statue occupies an honored spot.

After a quiet Christmas with his orphans in Savannah, the untiring evangelist left for Charlestown, where more trouble was awaiting him. As soon as he arrived, he was charged with having written a "false, malicious, scandalous, and infamous Libel against the Clergy." The truth was that Whitefield had edited a letter written by a certain Hugh Bryan criticizing American ministers. Whitefield answered the charge, agreeing to appear before the forthcoming general quarter sessions. Apparently the inhabitants of Charlestown did not share the clergy's hostility toward him, for by the time he sailed "over Charlestown Bar" on January 24, 1741, they had showered him with provisions for the long voyage. He docked at Falmouth on March 11 to find England hostile toward him. "Instead of having thousands to attend me," he relates, "scarce one of my spiritual children came to see me from morning to night . . ." Being George Whitefield, he was used to being the center of controversy, and such a state of affairs did not worry him unduly. Instead, he was much more interested in finding a soul-mate.

Whitefield needed a sensible wife to supervise the management of his orphanage, and his choice was a strong-minded widow, ten years his senior, Elizabeth Burnell James, of Abergavenny, Monmouthshire. They were married November 14, 1741, in St. Martin's Chapel, near Caerphilly. He described her then as "Once gay; but, for three years last past, a despised follower of the Lamb of God." To Gilbert Tennent, the Son of Thunder, he wrote that she was "neither rich in fortune, nor beautiful as to her person, but, I believe, a true child of God, and one who would not, I think, attempt to hinder me in His work for the world."

The *Gentleman's Magazine* differs with the bridegroom on the state of the widow's finances, stating that she not only was wealthy but had a dowry of ten thousand pounds, a large sum in those days.

John Wesley speaks of Mrs. Whitefield as being "a woman of candour and humanity." Whitefield terms her his "yoke-mate."

The Whitefields had one child, John, born on October 4, 1741, who died the following February. Whitefield, who had baptized the boy with such fatherly pride, now had to bury him.

"Last night," he sadly wrote, "I was called to sacrifice my Isaac; I mean to bury my only child and son about four months old." Mrs. Whitefield was left on her own for long periods of time while her husband was away preaching and she forwarded his mail to wherever he might be. When they were together she busied herself copying his letters.

Invited to Edinburgh by the "Associate Presbytery," who had recently seceded from the Church of Scotland, he incurred the enmity of its leaders because he would not ally himself absolutely with their cause. This did not prevent his preaching to any who would listen, and, upon leaving the city, to cry, "O Edinburgh, Edinburgh, surely thou wilt never be forgotten by me!" During his second visit made in 1742 the people mobbed him so that he was nearly "Hugged to death." That summer Whitefield actually preached in a tent erected by officials of Heriot's Hospital. This use of a tent for religious revivals heralded the tent services conducted by succeeding generations of American evangelists.

Turning to Calvinist teachings in Wales, Whitefield became moderator of the first Calvinistic Methodist Conference, and later was elected perpetual moderator.

An unfortunate disagreement with his former friend and teacher John Wesley occurred in 1741. The dispute concerned a sermon preached by Wesley entitled "Free Grace," which denied predestination. Whitefield, who believed his own destiny to have been ordained at birth by God Himself, answered the sermon in a public letter that caused a short break in the warm friendship between the two great evangelists. Wesley confessed that it was "not merely the difference of doctrine that caused the division, it was rather Mr. Whitefield's manner." Fortunately the two were reconciled in eighteen months, never to fall out again.

During the summer of 1744, Mr. and Mrs. Whitefield set out for America. Upon arrival Whitefield was taken so ill that he could not bear the visitors who came to pray with him. He was encouraged in his recovery by good news from Bethesda and the plantation he had bought with three hundred pounds given him by the good people of Charlestown. His pleasure was somewhat spoiled by the severe criticism meted out to him in various hostile publications by the somewhat jealous Reverend Charles Chauncy (1705-

1787) of Boston. Chauncy demanded to know what happened to Whitefield's "little flock" at the orphanage when he was engaged elsewhere in itinerant preaching. The attack may well have stemmed from those same unedited personal *Journals* printed without his consent that by their honesty and outspokenness had offended so many readers. In any case, Whitefield thanked God for the leisure afforded him upon the return journey to England when he was able to delete certain "excessive language" from unacceptable passages in readiness for reprinting. *He was also somewhat chastened.*

Whitefield's field preaching in Britain was interrupted by four other visits to America. Occasionally he was threatened with bodily harm by a mob. Once a man tried to stab him, while upon another occasion a tormentor flicked a long whip in his face all the while he was preaching. Yet toward the end of his life he could write, perhaps a little nostalgically, "There are few that like to go out into the fields; broken heads and dead cats are no more the ornaments of a Methodist, but silk scarves." Field preaching was always food and drink to George Whitefield.

Selina, Countess of Huntingdon, still continued to be his valued patroness. In spite of her religious "eccentricities," she was much respected by fellow aristocrats, who delighted in her baroque costumes of many colors. It was she who managed to persuade that same "Beau" Nash who had exchanged words with John Wesley to attend one of Whitefield's sermons. Unfortunately, the ensuing appearance of sarcastic puns about the Countess and Nash only resulted in Nash's vowing never to enter her house again.

When Lady Chesterfield, who had also met Whitefield through an introduction by the Countess, appeared dressed in somber brown at George II's naughty court, the King quipped, "I know who chose that gown for you—Mr. Whitefield!"

Of mixed Church of England and Dissenting views, the Countess of Huntingdon built several chapels in Southern England. She appointed Whitefield her domestic chaplain so that he was present with five other clerics at the dedication of the Bath edifice in 1765 which, according to a contemporary report, had the distinction of having "true Gothic windows." Equally popular now with the aristocracy, Whitefield preferred preaching to his beloved out-of-door congregations.

At the Countess' home the idea crystallized to replace a wooden building erected at Moorfields, London, by Whitefield's friends, with another of brick, to be known as the Tabernacle. "With awful solemnity," the first brick was laid in March of 1753.

In 1756 the famous Tottenham Court Road Chapel, for which Whitefield had collected 600 pounds, was built, together with twelve almshouses for the exclusive occupation of "godly widows," called by Whitefield his "life guards." "In those houses," he said, "I maintain twelve poor widows, and their prayers help to keep me alive."

Both the Tabernacle and Tottenham Court Road Chapel were, during the years that followed, to become famous as revered centers of Methodism. On Sunday, July 23, 1769, the ever-energetic Countess opened her chapel at Tunbridge Wells, where the previous year she had bought a house on fashionable Mount Ephraim. She sent out hundreds of invitations; yet the uninvited guests brought the most joy to the good woman, who was awakened early in the morning "by voices of praise" beneath her windows. The small wooden chapel could not hold so large a congregation, so that Whitefield, much to his delight, was obliged to conduct most of the service from an improvised pulpit in the chapel yard where, according to Kenneth Weller, "his text, 'how dreadful is this place,' bore no reference to the new building!"

Today the occasion is remembered by a stone pedestal placed on the spot with an inscription reading:

Near this spot
stood and preached
that eminent servant
of God
George Whitefield
at the opening of the original chapel
built by Selina
Countess of Huntingdon
July 23, 1769.

During his varied travels George Whitefield never forgot his Georgia lambs in the orphanage, at all times keeping up an individual correspondence with them. His letters would not have pleased our twentieth century child psychologists, although upon them the lambs seemed to have thrived. He wrote little Rebekah, for instance, "You may well wonder that God has not sent you to hell long ago."

When a new lamb arrived at Bethesda's ever-open doors the occupants chanted,

What tho' our Parents dear are dead,
Yet our great God provides;
Our Bodies here are cloth'd and fed;
Our Souls have Christian Guides.

Whitefield's devotion to charitable causes was amazing. He collected a "considerable Sum of Money" for those who suffered in the great Boston fire of 1760, and was accorded a vote of thanks by its inhabitants. He asked help to refurbish the burned-out library at Harvard University. "Mr. Wheelock's Indian School" similarly met with his support. Now even the students of Yale begged him "to give them one more quarter of an hour exhortation."

Whitefield's only major failure seems to have been his efforts to have Bethesda chartered as a college. Although supported by both houses of the Georgia Assembly, the plan never materialized, due to the insistence of the Archbishop of Canterbury and the president of the Privy Council that the college head must be a member of the Church of England.

In 1768, Mrs. Whitefield, after twenty-seven years of marriage to the evangelist, "was joyfully released," according to her epitaph in the Tottenham Court Road Chapel. Never was there a more uncomplaining wife, although she was left for months at a time by her wandering husband. After her demise he did admit that she had been his "right hand." The people of Virginia had found Elizabeth Whitefield "affable" and "well-bred."

As a husband, Whitefield was something of a perfectionist. Meals had to be served to the second; all papers and furniture had to be left in their exact place before he went to bed.

On November 30, 1769, Whitefield arrived in America for what proved to be the last time. Though suffering from an asthmatic condition, he enjoyed wintering at Bethesda, then went North to preach for the "thousands waiting to hear." Reaching the home of the Reverend Jonathan Parsons, the Presbyterian minister of Newburyport, Massachusetts, he preached, candle in hand, to the people gathered in front of his host's residence. Next morning at

six, George Whitefield, Evangelist, "fetched but one gasp
. . . and breathed no more."

When the news eventually reached England, John
Wesley preached for his friend an official funeral sermon in
both the Tabernacle and Tottenham Court Road Chapel.

Charles Wesley composed a poem:

> And is my WHITEFIELD entered into rest,
> With sudden death, with sudden glory blest?
> Left for a few sad moments here behind,
> I bear his image on my faithful mind.

Indeed, it was hard for the people of England and America to believe that the trumpeting voice of their common
evangelist was really stilled forever.

Chapter Two

"FATHER" DYER, THE SNOWSHOE ITINERANT

(1812=1901)

"It was my practice to go around the camps and invite all to come and hear the word. I would say to the boys at cards: 'Can't you get through with your game in twenty minutes, stack up your chips, and give us a hearing?' Frequently they would all come; and they always conducted themselves with propriety. Indeed, I never found it otherwise in these mountains."

Eight-year-old John Lewis Dyer could hardly wait for the toot of the horn signaling the opening of morning service. All week, as he helped his parents with the chores on their Ohio farmstead, his mind kept wandering to the exciting spectacle he would witness at church the follow-

ing Sunday. Eight bona fide Red Indians, newly converted
by the Methodists to the Christian faith, would be singing
hymns and giving testimonies.

The camp meeting service was to be held on Big Darby
Creek bottom in the Chenoweth settlement. There James
B. Finley was presiding elder, his duties including the evangelizing of the Indian Mission at Sandusky. He traveled a
large circuit, with his few valuables stashed away in his
saddlebag. John Lewis had often heard his parents speak
of the hardships endured by Finley and other preachers like
him. They were often compelled to swim swollen streams,
guiding their horse by a string behind them. Preaching
daily, they received no remuneration other than the food
and clothing provided by the faithful.

At last the Biblical horn was blown by a huge, red-
cheeked man who seemed to have the strength of an ox.
Wide-eyed, John Lewis watched for the Indians, but to
his keen disappointment, when they appeared they were
not dressed in legendary warpaint and feathers. Instead, they
wore white men's clothes—dismal black suits, checkered
pants, and large, wide-brimmed hats. Their straight black
hair had been neatly combed to their shoulders.

In spite of what he thought to be their "shortcomings,"
John Lewis never forgot the way they sang the hymn in
their own tongue without benefit of book or note:

> O happy are they, who their Savior obey,
> And have laid up their treasure above!

Camp-meeting season was an eagerly awaited time in the
hard, toil-filled lives of these pioneer Americans. Today,
when churches and synagogues openly advertise air-con-
ditioned places of worship, one might well recall those
hardy forebears who in summer braved sun and mosquitoes

to attend open-air revivals. The coming of the presiding elder for Quarterly Meeting was the sign of Pentecost.

Finley, himself the son of "fire-and-brimstone" preacher Robert W. Finley, was a handsome man then in the prime of life. In John Lewis' estimation, "he [Finley] seemed to move heaven and earth. The Holy Spirit was poured out, and scores were crying for mercy, and as many others shouting the praise of God. Some were stricken down with conviction, and lay like dead men, but would come to life again, shouting happily."

Such visible expressions were quite common. Young Dyer's parents called them "the jerks," declaring they had first occurred in Kentucky. Actually, in varying forms such peculiar physical phenomena have been known to exist through the ages. The Dyers recalled a certain camp-meeting at Cane Ridge held by Presbyterians and Methodists where men and women "fell by the score." When some of them failed to "recover" from their stupor, a doctor was called. Setting to work with his smelling salts (known as hartshorn) he, himself, was caught in the religious frenzy and fell down too!

John Lewis Dyer was born on March 16, 1812, at the junction of the Darbys, Franklin County, Ohio, where in 1800, on a tract of land containing six hundred acres, his grandfather John Dyer had built the first grist mill in Central Ohio.

Samuel Dyer, John Lewis' father, had married Cassandra Foster, daughter of Lewis Foster, a local Methodist preacher, in October, 1810. In addition to being a farmer, Samuel was a justice of the peace, holding his own primitive court where the chief offenders were drunkards. One of them insisted upon shaking hands with John Lewis, then four years old, and when the child drew away, shouted, "That child will make a drunkard as sure as he lives. I have never see a child that hated a drunken man but would surely be a drunkard." Unconsciously he had done the child a favor. Badly frightened, the little boy never forgot the awful prophecy.

Life on a pioneer farm was a hard but happy one. The land had to be cleared of trees and underbrush before cultivation could begin. When John Lewis grew big enough to reach the plow handles, he was put to plowing. "If I had not gone at least two rounds across a ten-acre field before sunrise, it was thought a late start," he says.

School was only held during three of the winter months when his studies included "the three R's and orthography." Spelling contests between neighboring schools created as much excitement as the football games of today. Dyer described such a match in his memoirs. "The school on Glade Run and ours once met halfway. Each side put up its picked ten. We were gaining rapidly, when the man who gave out the words was caught cheating us. This raised quite a disturbance; but we chose a man who lived on their side, in whose honesty we had confidence, and the contest went on, our side winning and my brother Robert bearing off the honors."

When he was eighteen years old, John Lewis was sent by his parents to study mathematics "with a Mr. Phelps, the county surveyor" thirty miles away in the "Big Woods" of Marysville, Union County. During the four months' sojourn there, he thoroughly enjoyed this variation from farming chores. "I went as a hand occasionally," he wrote, "and thus secured practice as well as theory. This was of advantage to me in early times in Illinois."

Two years earlier, the first Sunday school had been organized in the vicinity of the Dyer farm, where lessons consisted mainly "of learning and reciting chapters of the New Testament." Commented John Lewis, "Outside of the large towns, Central Ohio was slow in planting Sunday schools."

Life on the old frontier was not all hard work and studying. The favorite form of relaxation for John Lewis and his younger brother Robert was hunting. The forests around their log home abounded in wild turkeys, deer and raccoons. "Every boy was familiar with the use of the rifle —old-fashioned muzzle-loaders, powder-horn and charger, and patch and ball, and flintlock."

Whenever there was a shortage of acorns, their staple food, hungry raccoons ravaged the Dyer fields. Such times provided good sport for John Lewis and Robert. With horse and 'coon dog they would set out upon a raccoon hunt, seldom returning empty-handed. "We used no guns; but would tree the 'coon, climb after him, shake him off, and leave the dog to make the finish, which was not always an easy task, as the 'coon was capable of making an obstinate fight. . . . Coon skins were like currency on the frontier, selling for twenty-five cents apiece. When we counted seven as the result of a single hunt, Robert and I felt 'passing rich.' "

During the fall of 1831, when John Lewis was in his twentieth year, the family decided to move to the prairies of Illinois "as far as the Illinois River." Being the eldest of a family that now boasted eight children, John Lewis drove the larger of the two wagons, which was pulled by four horses.

Because the summer had been unusually wet, the muddy tracks slowed the wagons' speed considerably. Sometimes they took an entire week to cover forty-five miles. John Lewis recalled that, under the circumstances, the chief topic of conversation among the teams was understandably MUD. One settler declared: "All that you have seen is nothing. I was looking ahead and saw a plug hat on the mud, and thought I had a prize. As I got nearer, it seemed to have a man's head in it, which said, 'Let me alone, I have a good horse under me!' "

The Dyer family finally settled in the vicinity of Canton, Illinois. During 1831 Black Hawk (1767-1838), famed chief of the Sac and Fox Indians, attacked the white settlers, and John Lewis joined the other young men who had volunteered their services as rangers to help subdue him. When Black Hawk and his band were whipped, fifty miles of territory were ceded to the United States on the west side of the Mississippi River.

Because of the richness of its soil, Illinois proved to be a place of opportunity for new settlers. Property was at a premium; speculation ran high. Then in 1837 came the great financial crash that shook the entire nation. Times were hard for the Dyer family. Once John Lewis hauled a load of wheat thirty-five miles to Peoria to find it priced at only 25 cents a bushel. "Everything," he said, "but the churches stood still. The Methodist Church was far in the lead."

Religious conviction had troubled John Lewis Dyer for some time. He felt that "a heavy cloud" of sin was stifling him; that somehow it had to be lifted. John Lewis was sure in his heart that "through Christ's all-cleansing blood" God had something wonderful in store for him. His parents were God-fearing people and he longed to emulate them.

There was no regular circuit preaching in the northern part of Fulton County where his family were located until the fall of 1832. Two years before, his name had been put forward as "a seeker on probation" when he made what he described as "my first public attempt to seek the salvation of my soul." The peace of mind he thought he had found disappeared temporarily when he was tempted to join other young people at social gatherings in "innocent plays."

Upon his return from fighting Black Hawk, John Lewis prayed constantly for guidance in religious matters. By his own account, he was kneeling one day by the root of an aged tree, where "just behind me I heard a voice, saying: 'Your work is not done; go ye into all the world and preach the gospel.' "

John Lewis, aware from childhood of the hard and penurious lot of the circuit preacher, had often exclaimed that he would rather be anything "than a poor Methodist preacher." Instead, he consented to become a "licensed exhorter" and a circuit steward.

Exhorting did not unduly distract him from the important business of courting Harriet Foster, youngest daughter of Zebulon Foster, one of the first settlers at Fort Washington, now Cincinnati. At the same time on December 4, 1833, Zebulon's youngest son married John Lewis' eldest sister. The Dyers had five children, three boys and two girls. In 1844 they left Illinois to settle in Potosi, Wisconsin, where John Lewis, tiring of farming, decided to try prospecting in the lead mines, with some luck. With several hundred dollars in the bank, the future seemed bright for the Dyers when suddenly on July 14, 1847, Harriet died. Two months later she was followed by their thirteen-months-old daughter.

Prosperous but lonely, it was little wonder John Lewis fell prey to the charms of a talkative lady who conveniently omitted telling him that she had married two husbands already, one of whom was still alive. Going to the altar for the third time, she therefore contracted a bigamous marriage with John Lewis who, when he found out, applied for a separation. In spite of the doubtful validity of the marriage, he was forced publicly to "divorce" the talkative lady in Lancaster, Grant County, Wisconsin.

Feeling spiritually tarnished, John Lewis asked his preacher and a committee of fellow church members to investigate the case, as he was then classleader, and wished to exonerate his church of any responsibility. They in turn acquitted him of all guilt in the sorry matter.

Moving with his young family to Lost Grove, Wisconsin, he continued lead prospecting. He was now in financial distress, his second "wife" having spent all of his savings. His sister Rachel kept house while his brother Robert, his favorite childhood companion, arrived to help him prospect.

Moving again, this time to Mineral Point, John Lewis was persuaded by fellow Methodists to try his voice at preaching. Unfortunately he became tongue-tied before his first congregation and had to sit down without uttering a word. The following Sunday night he tried again, telling the congregation, "I suppose you all remember last Sunday night's failure; but I am not convinced that there is no preach in me yet."

This time John Lewis successfully gave a sermon, later being asked to become a supply circuit preacher. He declined, preferring to set out for his Yellow Stone Mine. On the way his horse went wild and "tore almost everything to pieces." John Lewis had a remarkable escape from injury.

Next day, while working thirty feet down a mine shaft, he was overcome with a suffocating feeling of guilt, so that his lungs seemed ready to burst. "Oh Lord, what ails me?" he managed to cry. Suddenly the memory of the voice he had heard long before by the tree rushed through his mind. To no avail he had then been told to go and preach the gospel; now once more he had refused the call.

Dramatically putting down his pick and shovel, John Lewis Dyer left the pit forever. Back at their little cabin, he told Robert, "I am going to try to preach the gospel." Robert's only reply was to remind him of Davy Crockett's famous quotation: "Be sure you're right, then go ahead."

The presiding elder sent the new preacher to work with the Reverend A. H. Walter on the Wingville and Lancaster circuit. This was a real trial of courage. As there was no church building, Dyer was obliged to give a sermon in the very courthouse where six months previously he had divorced "that woman." None of the good-natured congregation seemed to hold this against him, however, so he "thanked God and took courage."

"That woman," like Lot's wife, came to an untimely end. She was living at Snake Hollow, Wisconsin, when a cloudburst caused a sudden flood. Alarmed, she ran to a neighbor until, as she thought, danger was over, but upon her return journey she became entangled in some driftwood. Next morning she was found in a whirlpool of water, by a streak of irony being the only person drowned in the flood.

For ten years from 1851, Dyer worked as a circuit preacher in various parts of Wisconsin and Minnesota, during which time he was to know varied hardships and adventures.

Because he was a widower, John Lewis received only a single man's pay of a hundred dollars per quarter for his preaching work. With four children, one of them crippled from "white swelling," and his sister Rachel to care for, living was not easy.

On one occasion smallpox and then cholera broke out in the confines of his circuit. At Wiota an entire family died, whereupon the congregation burned the dead in the house. "This was before the days of cremation, so far as I know," noted Dyer, "or it would not have looked so horrible."

The sheer terror of such sudden plagues in pioneer townships Dyer graphically noted.

Brother and Sister Benson, both members of our Church, were called away. The mother was taken first. I visited her. She was in extreme pain, but was resigned to the will of God. In twenty-four hours she died. I was with her to the last. It was warm weather, and at nine o'clock in the evening we sent out for help, as she was a large woman. Only Aunt Polly Journey came. My sister was at home with my sick daughter, and I sent for her. Nathan Woodberry also came, and as the bedroom was too small, we carried the corpse out in front of the house, and laid her out. Two or three had been dispatched to dig the grave. Her husband had sent to have a coffin, as he feared the people would want to bury her without one. But he need not have feared, for scarcely one could be got near the house. Mr. Woodberry got a wagon and team, and we went a half mile for the coffin. It was not quite done. This was Monday night, and I tried to preach three times the day before. I lay down in the shavings and slept till the coffin was done, when I was awaked and ready for service. About day-break there were just enough of us to perform the burial of the poor woman so suddenly called to death. Just before she breathed her last, the little boy was taken down, and within twenty-four hours he was buried. I was not there, as I had been called to attend a funeral.

John Lewis' preaching was sincere enough, although his voice did not always please his flock. "You read and let your sister pray; she don't pray quite so loud as you do," one outspoken man told him.

Often at camp revival meetings gangs of rowdies would try to break up the harmony of the proceedings. On one such occasion John Lewis heard a large man crowing like a rooster. When he struck the preacher, the rooster-man got more than he bargained for: ". . . without thought my fist struck on the left arm, met his eye, and he was just down and I had him by the throat," recorded John Lewis.

"Don't hurt him," wailed Brother Moore, a local minister.

"God have mercy on him," yelled John Lewis, "for it is hard for me, too."

A few days after the fighting preacher had been appointed to Richland Mission, Fillmore County, Minnesota, his sister married a Dr. W. B. Thurston. John Lewis with his eldest son, Joshua, traveled by mule, buggy and steamboat to his new circuit. The son later left for St. Paul to find himself an opening in business. At this time personal sorrow came to John Lewis when his brother Robert accidentally shot himself.

John Lewis wrote, "My fifteen-year-old daughter and Samuel, my twelve-year-old son, kept house in our cabin, a mile from neighbours and alone when I was on the circuit. Daughter says that I left no latch on the door, and that she cries from fear at night."

Her father does not appear to have worried unduly about this, as he noted with the optimism characteristic of his era, "But our God seldom, if ever, permits evil to befall us or our families if we keep on preaching the gospel."

John Lewis suffered in the further financial crash of 1857 when together with several others he stood security for a man who promised to bring a sawmill into his circuit area. The man defaulted. Still receiving a single man's salary,

John Lewis, after this loss, could never recoup his resources. His health suffered; circuit work was hard. He wrote, "New, rough, timbered country, with times hard and many of the people poor." Finally, his eyes were smitten with a terrible soreness. "I still kept up my work until April; not able to read—could hardly read my letters; stood in front of the light at night; had the lids of my eyes turned over and burnt with caustic, and concluded to quit and rest awhile."

At Lenora, Minnesota, the oldest church in Fillmore County has a plaque to his memory, while local historical records note that

> Rev. John Dyer, rough, uncouth, eccentric, was one of the noblest soldiers of the cross who ever set foot in Fillmore County. He labored in the vicinity for six years. Undaunted by hardships, this valiant Christian, wearing a dilapidated plug hat, presenting with gaunt, strong, rugged physique, a strange picture on his raw-boned horse, rode his circuits enduring untold hardships and deprivations, serving his people wherever he found them. When he came to Minnesota he had $1,600.00, but in going security for the notes in the upbuilding of the church and of the Lenora village, he lost it all.

Recovering at last both from his ailment and its painful treatment, he gathered together a few belongings in a carpet-sack, including "a Bible, hymn book, Discipline of our Church, and a copy of Lorain's Sea Sermons, with a change of linen, and fourteen dollars and seventy-five cents in silver and gold."

Then he set out alone upon "a splendid riding animal" for what was to be his greatest earthly adventure—Pike's Peak!

In 1858, toward summer's end, word had leaked out that gold had been discovered in the Pike's Peak region. The value of the finds snowballed, causing men impoverished by the panic of 1857 to set out by covered wagon and horseback, and even on foot, for the bleak, barren mountainsides. Clerks, lawyers and doctors mingled with farm workers toiling footsore, hungry and often in rags across the endless prairie. Death came to many when they ran out of food; even cannibalism was not unknown. The covered wagons brazenly flaunted the message "Pike's Peak or Bust." Unfortunately, many of them were busted in the effort, for they soon discovered that expensive machinery was the only adequate way to extract the precious metal from the Rockies. Absentee owners, corporate companies and professional engineers were eventually to supplant the eager prospector with his pick and washing-pan. Of course there were some who really did become rich overnight with a lucky strike, but they were in the minority.

John Lewis hoped to meet one of his sons who had made the journey west a year before. Before leaving, he vowed to pay back every cent owing in debts.

His eyes were not fully recovered, a fact that worried his other children and friends, but he told them that he had a bottle of Sloan's Instant Relief with which to wipe his eyes open every morning.

Leaving Minnesota after six years, he reflected happily that in that time he had seen "over five hundred penitents" at the altar, ". . . most of whom had professed conversion." In some parts of his circuit he had actually been the first preacher. There had even been some missionary work among the Chippewa Indians.

Two days after starting out he was forced to abandon

his splendid mount, for an irate landlord, whose pet sitting hen she had disturbed, shut her in a stall covered with a peck of corn where "she was foundered almost to death." Sadly, the poor preacher sold her for fifteen dollars plus a gun and an old watch—"a very little more than the saddle and bridle were worth."

Continuing on foot to Omaha, he heard of a train of eighteen wagons that were about to leave for Pike's Peak. In return for the fifteen dollars, one of the wagon owners agreed to board him and haul his carpet-sack, stipulating however that the preacher himself would have to walk!

That Sunday John Lewis was asked to preach at the afternoon service in Fremont, the last settlement between the Missouri River and the Rocky Mountains. Thinking he could easily catch up with an ox team, he agreed. There were thirty in the congregation. The next morning, thanks to his "strong walking legs," he easily rejoined the train.

At Fort Kearney he took several five-mile trips to the Bluffs for, as he said, "I wanted to see a buffalo, but never got sight of one, much less a chance to shoot one." He did, however, see Indians, bitterly complaining that "the poor creatures had learned to swear." Of their eating habits he noted, "A fat dog belonging to the train began to stagger, and soon died. It was thought he got strychnine. The Indians saw him kicking his last, and offered twenty-five cents for him. They skinned and cooked him, and soon had dog-soup."

During the long journey John Lewis proved—as he had done with the rooster-man—that he was no coward. A drunken man ran into the oxen's corral swearing he would have beef for supper. As he lifted a gun to prove his point, the preacher was the only member of the wagon train

man enough to challenge him. Raising a big ox-gad (goad),
he ordered the intruder to get out fast, which he did. The
Reverend Dyer was hero of the hour.

Footsore and bored by the long, uneventful journey,
John Lewis finally arrived at Cherry Creek, two miles
above Denver. His last remaining two dollars and fifty cents
had been stolen from his pants during the last night spent on
the plains. He found his son, visited with him for a few
hours, and promptly announced that he intended to continue his preaching. The next Sunday he gave his first
sermon in Colorado at the invitation of the Reverend William A. Kenny, newly arrived minister of the Methodist
Episcopal Church. His subject was repentance with some
patriotism thrown in for good measure, the Civil War
having recently begun.

Hearing that exciting things were happening in Buckskin
Joe, John Lewis quickly made up his mind to go there at
once. The Phillips Lode was experiencing a gold boom that
was somewhat unique of its kind, being worked like a
quarry.

John Lewis joined up with a company whose team
hauled his meager belongings while he again walked by the
side. By his standards—having walked half across a continent—the distance of 100 miles was comparatively short.

Arriving at Buckskin Joe on July 9, John Lewis found
the bonanza settlement invigorating and lively. Just two
months after leaving Lenora, Minnesota, he felt in good
health. Even his eyes showed improvement. Inquiring into
local religious matters, he found that Brother William How-
bert had conducted a funeral in 1860, and Brother William
Antis had held one service.

This was all the incentive that Brother Dyer wanted. In

no time he was preaching at the street corners. On the first Sunday in August he walked eight miles to Montgomery only to find a congregation of one man. All the others were out staking claims. The man asked him to stay to dinner. Says John Lewis in *The Snow-Shoe Itinerant*, "We sat down on the ground to eat, as there was not a house, table, or stool, in the place."

On the twenty-fifth of the month he was off to Mosquito, where after building himself a pine-bough shelter, he preached the first sermon ever heard there. He stayed for nine weeks before setting out to California Gulch, where his services in taking charge of the mission had been requested by the pastor who supplied it. According to his own account, the presiding elder, John M. Chivington, had become a major in the army, and "I was left on my own resources in a wilderness country, with six or seven members, and they scattered over one hundred miles!"

Pack on back, he slowly picked his way for eight miles up the range to the top of the Mosquito Pass, "the highest and hardest range I had then crossed," preaching that night at California Gulch. Next day he was marching along an old Indian trail to the Gunnison country. Taking off his boots, he waded the Arkansas River where he thought that "the cold water would cut my legs off." For the first time he saw the fabled Twin Lakes. Snowy mountain ranges and unspoiled wilderness lay on either side.

The next day at Kent's Gulch he found about a hundred men. Only one had a family, and he was just putting a roof of poles, grass and earth on his rough house. When Dyer said that he was "a bit of a Methodist preacher" and asked if he might preach in that house, the reply was, "You can, sir, when I get the roof on." There were only two benches inside, and when the time came, they were filled. The overflow crowd had to "sit on the dirt floor, in rows facing one another, knee to knee." Nobody seemed to mind the preacher's loud voice as he roared out a sermon entitled "Repentance and Conversion." It was the first ever given in the Gunnison country. A collection amounting to twenty dollars was taken.

Off again the next morning, Dyer made for Washington Gulch, forty-five miles west, passing Deadman's Gulch, where only in 1859 the Indians had killed six would-be fortune hunters. Bones of men and horses lay bleaching in the sun.

When John Lewis finally reached Minersville, Washington Gulch, on Sunday, September 24, he found that nobody was respecting the Sabbath. "One man was cutting and selling wood; others rolling logs and selling beef; others rolling logs down the hill; others covering their cabins; another building a chimney; and still others selling provisions and whisky in a tent. From this standpoint I resolved to announce my appointment."

Hailing one fellow who was dressing some grouse, John Lewis asked, "Did you not expect a Methodist preacher would be on hand as soon as you had chicken to eat?"

The man winked an eye as he replied, "Well, I have heard that they were fond of chicken." Then he extended the new preacher an invitation to share them.

First, however, there was religious business to be attended to. Stepping to the middle of the camp, John Lewis shouted like a town crier, "O yes! O yes! There will be preaching at half past ten o'clock wherever the most people can be found together."

They were found around the grocery tent, forty men,

jacks and ponies. Standing at the open flap, the new preacher began to half sing, half read the words of the hymn, "Alas! and did my Savior bleed?" In twos and threes the customers joined in, while all the time the business of buying and selling provisions continued unheeded. But when John Lewis' cannonlike voice boomed out the order, "Let us pray," everybody stopped what he was doing and bowed his head. After that, all was plain sailing, except for the fact that during the sermon a mule stuck its head into the tent and made off with a loaf of bread.

That night a revival meeting was held around the campfires, light being provided by pine knots. It was an all-male gathering for, according to John Lewis, there was only one woman living within a radius of a hundred miles.

Retracing his steps along the Indian trail on Tuesday morning, the preacher met a German in Deadman's Gulch, who, asking for the history of the tragic bones, whipped his jackass and made off at a gallop when Dyer told him the story of the massacre.

Later, coming across a Southerner, the preacher, although unarmed, boldly announced that he was for the Union. The other man, though armed, suggested they "talk friendly on the subject." They did, parting still friendly the next morning after passing a night under the same tree.

At Kent Gulch, he married a runaway couple from Denver. The bride was only sixteen. Off again on his new circuit, he passed through Georgia Bar on the Arkansas River, where some fifty men were panning out dust. Passing a lonely cabin, he was asked if he was the man who had preached below the previous night. If so, would he conduct the funeral of a young man who had died suddenly?

John Lewis reported, "I felt gloomy. . . . Forty men and two women were present. All seemed to be deeply affected, as it was the first funeral most of us had been at in the mountains. He was buried as decently as the circumstances would admit."

After another visit to California Gulch, the preacher was back at Gunnison again where, joining up with a Noah Armstrong, he decided to do some prospecting himself. They bought a jack, working for three weeks unsuccessfully before a deep snowfall halted their operations.

Seventy miles from suitable winter quarters, the pair started out in snow from three to five feet deep. Walking on short rations, sometimes they "shoveled snow for three days and a half to get three and a half miles." On Sunday they stopped while John Lewis, at Noah's request, preached a sermon on the Prodigal Son. Then they crossed the main range.

"I reached California Gulch in good health, weighed one hundred and sixty-three pounds, and when I left the States, pulled one hundred and ninety-two pounds. I found out that a man at forty-seven, getting fat, could walk, work, and preach off all the fat."

After ten days of meetings, the inhabitants grumbled that they "must have the school house to dance in," so the preacher had to yield. John Lewis returned alone to Buckskin Joe by way of Weston Pass. It was a fearsome journey. At timber height he ran into a bad blizzard. His box of matches would not light; for six hours he plodded through waist-deep snow. It was after dark when finally he reached the toll gate, where he was befriended by a kindly Swede. Soon recovered from his ordeal, he was off as fast as his legs could carry him to Fairplay, preaching at Sharman's

Store. Back in Buckskin Joe, he held a two-week revival with Brother Antis, where they had plenty of competition, or "opposition," as he called it, in "two balls a week, a dancing school, a one-horse theater and two men shot."

In four months John Lewis had mushed his way five hundred miles over Indian trails carrying a heavy pack and preaching, on an average, three times a week. Collections made a grand total of forty-three dollars, whereas nothing he could find to eat cost less than twenty-five cents a pound. His clothes were threadbare, his hat patched with dressed antelope skin, and his shoes half-soled with raw hide. Notwithstanding, "Father" Dyer, as the miners had affectionately dubbed him, was an exceedingly happy man.

Around February 1, John Lewis, minus the ten dollars fare on the weekly coach, set out to attend the missionary conference in Denver. He covered the hundred or so miles in two and a half days. Dressed like a miner, without a vest, he secluded himself at the back of the hall only to be spotted by the former presiding elder, now Colonel John Chivington, resplendent in military uniform complete with bowie-knife and revolver.

Marching down the aisle, Chivington caught hold of John Lewis by the scruff of his neck, bluntly ordering, "Come, preach for me." Knowing that "it was always best for me to whet my own scythe," John Lewis did as he was told, soon forgetting his poor clothes.

At the end of March, "Father" Dyer was appointed by the Kansas Conference, of which the Rocky Mountain district then formed part, to look after Blue River Mission in Summit County.

Once more, because of lack of funds, he was obliged to go on foot, traveling by way of Central City. He crossed the range on a snow path, the drifts on either side being from five to fifteen feet deep. During the morning of April 2 he preached to one hundred and fifty people in Georgia Gulch, and in the afternoon to forty at French Gulch. Incensed at the preacher's poverty, a friendly Jew took up a collection amounting to $22.50 in gold dust, then accepted as currency in those parts. Dyer had arrived that day with only a dime in his pocket.

With an appropriation of $125 promised from the Conference, John Lewis felt himself unable to afford boarding rates in that expensive mountain country. Board cost $7 a week, the boarder having to provide his bed and do his own washing. He decided to buy a small cabin in French Gulch where the bedstead and springs were made of pine poles. For study material in addition to his Bible hymn book and Methodist Discipline, he read the *Rocky Mountain News* "to keep up with the times."

Covering the dirt floor with gunny sacks, he "preached to the people in my own house, not in a hired house, as the Apostle Paul did."

Making himself a pair of snowshoes, which in time were to earn him the nickname of "the Snowshoe Itinerant," he learned by trial and error to use them, often disappearing under a mound of snow. The mining congregation were friendly, treating him "and the cause of Christ" with respect.

Describing his flock, John Lewis said, "They were generally liberal, although it was not the custom always to pass the hat, and sometimes the preacher, when his pants began to wear out, would think the boys rather long between collections."

During the bitter winter months some of the congregation would leave for Denver and some for home. Many never returned with the spring thaw. "Father" Dyer complained of a troop of theatrical performers who played to all the camps on Sundays: "I thought the devil was travelling the circuit as well as myself."

Dyer always traveled the roads unarmed, although violent deaths from man or beast were frequent. Even when he slept in the open he seems never to have been bothered by Rocky Mountain lions or bears. Between sermons, the energetic parson augmented his income by digging, usually without success.

Dyer told many amusing stories of his "mountain folk." In one cabin he asked a married woman of forty if she had ever had a "religious experience," to which she gladly volunteered that she belonged to the Baptists. Somewhat bluntly John Lewis said that he would be glad to see a member of any church at this meeting. Couldn't she come and help? She declined with thanks, "because she was taking her first lessons in dancing."

Dyer hated dancing, which he considered the root of all evil. "People," he declared, "must not expect anything from a preacher but opposition to dancing, since John the Baptist lost his head through the flirtations of a silly girl."

But he was faithful to his scattered flock in spite of their "little regard" for "sacred things." This last complaint concerned his small portable organ, which they liked to borrow when he wasn't looking, to provide accompaniment for their dancing.

With Buckskin Joe as his base for spiritual operations, Dyer had a grueling Sunday schedule that did not vary, summer or winter. The day would begin with an early service at Fairplay, followed—after a ten-mile walk—by one at Buckskin Joe. Then came another ten-mile hike so that Montgomery could have a sermon at noon. Another twenty miles and he had crossed the Continental Divide, some 14,000 feet high, to give Breckenridge the evening meeting!

His evangelism was of the hell and brimstone variety. Either a man was saved or he wasn't. There were no half measures. In the rough mining communities, where a human life meant little and sudden death was a daily occurrence, "Father" Dyer fought to save for eternity the human soul.

For him there was little hope of great financial remuneration or the kind of fame that have been the earthly rewards of other evangelists both before and after him. He was a plain, old-fashioned preacher doing the best for his isolated mountain flock.

Still poorly paid, he was forced at one point to take a weekday job delivering the mail from Buckskin Joe to Cache Creek, taking in California Gulch. His forty-odd-mile journey earned him the princely sum of $18 per week. Between deliveries, he preached to the miners. Often he carried gold dust for the various camps on the upper Arkansas.

Once, after his feet had suffered from frost-bite, he noted:

'Uncle Tommy Cummings' brought a little balsam sapling, and we shaved off the bark, and poulticed both of my feet. The third week I was able to carry the mail. Half my toenails sloughed off, with considerable of the skin. For two weeks I was confined to the house, busying myself reading and doctoring my feet. I sent to H. A. W. Tabor, our storekeeper—now ex-Senator—and paid him sixteen cents a pound for corn to make hominy, which I considered a luxury.

The General Conference of 1868 sent "Father" Dyer to New Mexico, where, as usual, he ran into plenty of excitement. He wrote, "The Apache Indians were frequently on the scout. If sighted by them it was necessary to outrun them, kill them, or get scalped."

He found the Mexicans "a kind sympathetic people" and who would divide anything with a stranger. Before returning to Colorado he had covered ten thousand miles on horseback, preaching all the way.

On November 7, 1870, Dyer, a widower for over twenty years, married Mrs. Lucinda P. Rankin of Cherry Creek, Douglas County, Colorado. "Since I could almost keep myself, I thought it was a poor woman who could not help a little," he hopefully wrote, while contemplating his third trip to the altar. The third Mrs. Lewis made an admirable partner, who completely obliterated the sour memory of her predecessor.

"Father" Dyer gave his name to Dyersville, now a ghost-town in Summit County. His son, Probate Judge Elias F. Dyer, was shot by assassins in his own court room at Granite, Colorado, July 3, 1875. The youngest son, Samuel, lost a foot in the War between the States, while his eldest, Joshua, serving with the First Minnesota Regiment, perished when the steamship *General Lyon* was blown up off Cape Hatteras.

"Father" Dyer's third marriage was a happy one, although for a time his bride did have to live in a make-do parsonage at the back of a bowling alley. She died suddenly on April 9, 1888. Her widower continued preaching to "tie-cutters, wood-haulers, coke-burners and miners, in private houses, stores and school-houses, where my hearers frequently told me that it was the first preaching they had heard for two, three and five years."

Like the Biblical patriarchs, he lived to a ripe old age. He was nearly ninety years old when he died in Denver, June 15, 1901. His name is enshrined in marble at the state capital in Denver.

Chapter Three

MISTER MOODY

Dwight Lyman Moody

(1837=1899)

"Oh, the town's upside down, everybody seems mad.
When they come to their senses we all shall feel glad,
For the rich and the poor, and the good and the bad,
Are gone mad over Moody and Sankey."

> *Broad sheet sold in the Bull Ring,*
> *Birmingham, England,* 1875.

To welcome him into the world, Paul Revere's bell was rung in the meetinghouse steeple on the night Dwight Lyman Moody was born. He was the sixth child of Edwin and Betsey Moody, poverty-stricken residents of Northfield, Massachusetts, where their forebears had lived for several generations. Only a year before, the Bank of the United States had ceased operations, and in common with thousands of other families across the nation, the Moodys had had to mortgage their clapboard homestead. It was not the best of times for a baby to be born.

In addition to caring for the few animals he possessed, Edwin Moody—when so inclined—worked as stonemason and bricklayer. He was popular, if somewhat lazy, and his wife adored him. She overlooked his fondness for the whisky which was no good for his ailing heart.

On May 28, 1841, when Dwight Lyman was only four, his father was taken sick while bricklaying in town. He managed to reach home, where his wife discovered him slumped forward as if praying by the side of their bed. At forty-one Ed Moody was dead.

In June, his widow, Betsey, gave birth to twins, Sam and Lizzie. She now had nine mouths to feed and no money, for Edwin had died completely bankrupt.

As if this were not enough, Richard Colton, the chief creditor, claimed everything he could lay hands on, including the firewood. He even took the horse and buggy. The Moody boys did manage to hide their father's tools and one calf.

Wealthy Ezra Purple, waving a mortgage paper to the homestead, went so far as to invade the privacy of Betsey's bedroom, where she was confined, still weak from giving birth to the twins.

Charles Holton, her brother, describes the scene:

> Betsey wasn't up since the birth of her twins but she had him come to her bedroom, and told him that the money was not ready, but she would get it for him as soon as she could. Purple expressed his disappointment in unkind language, and soon left the house. Going down the hill the harness broke and he was thrown out on the ground—uninjured. Some of the townspeople, knowing the reason for his visit to Betsey, were so unkind as to say, "It was a pity he didn't break his neck." Hearing of

the straits Betsey was in, Cyrus and I, the two brothers living near her, managed to raise the money that year.

Ironically, some forty years later Dwight Lyman Moody was to take a Biblical-type revenge upon the Purple family.

Betsey's cup of woe was far from empty for, at fifteen years old, the eldest boy, Isaiah—her favorite child and mainstay—ran away. Dwight later realized that "all at once that boy became a wanderer. He had been reading some of the trashy novels, and the belief seized him that he had only to go away to make a fortune."

Positive that one day her first-born would return, Betsey, her hair prematurely turned white, each night placed a light for him in the window. Her faith that her prayers would be answered proved an inspiration to Dwight. He wrote:

> I can remember how eagerly she used to look for tidings of that boy; how she used to send us to the post office to see if there was a letter from him . . . to come back with the sad news, "no letter" . . . in the evenings we used to sit beside her . . . and talk about our father; but the moment the name of that boy was mentioned she would hush us into silence. Some nights when the wind was very high, and the house . . . would tremble at every gust, the voice of my mother was raised in prayer for that wanderer . . . Thanksgiving Day she set a chair for him, thinking he would return home.

Betsey's premonition proved correct. Her prodigal son did eventually return. Dwight records the scene:

> While my mother was sitting at the door, a stranger was seen coming toward the house, and when he came to the door he stopped. My mother didn't know her boy. He stood there with folded arms and a great beard flowing

down his breast, his tears trickling down his face. When my mother saw those tears she cried, "Oh, it's my lost son!" and entreated him to come in. But he stood still!

"No, Mother," replied the wanderer. "I will not come in until I hear first that you have forgiven me."

The widow was only too willing. . . . Dwight notes that "she rushed to the threshold, threw her arms around him, and breathed forgiveness."

Life for Dwight Moody during his childhood might not have been easy, but it had its lighter side. Although he had to save his footwear and stockings for Sunday use only, and exist for days on corn meal and milk, there were compensations.

There was sledding in winter, while in fall clubbing apples from neighbors' orchards proved tasty fun. Full of mischief, indoors and out, he was often punished by the Widow Moody. "Mother would send me out for a stick, and I thought I could fool her and get a dead one. But she would snap the stick and then tell me to get another. She was rarely in a hurry, and certainly never when she was whipping me. Once I told her that the whipping did not hurt . . . never again!"

A natural bargainer, Dwight once swapped Betsey's old swayback farm horse with a band of wandering gypsies for a fine young filly sporting a docked tail. His mother's reaction to this Yankee bargain is unfortunately not recorded for posterity.

Although she herself found no time to attend church, Betsey made sure that her offspring offset the omission. Says Dwight, "My mother started me off to Sunday school, and kept me going, and it was not to one service only, but to three. I went to church and heard the sermon; went to the graveyard where my father was buried and ate a little lunch that I took in my pocket; went back to Sunday school, and after Sunday school went to church again."

By his own confession, he approached Sunday with "a certain amount of dread." In addition to schooling, after working all his spare time on the farm, he found it hard to be obliged to go to church and hear a sermon he didn't understand. Of the parson he comments, "I don't know that the minister even noticed me, unless it was when I was asleep in the gallery, and he woke me up."

Of the three services, Dwight liked Sunday school best, especially when the superintendent had the good sense to wear down some of his excess energy by sending him out recruiting new members.

Dwight did not much care for ordinary school, or the rattan that went with it, and his spelling and grammar left much to be desired.

When he was ten years old, his mother was obliged to "let him out to a farmer."

My brother introduced me to the old man and his wife with whom I was to live. I was to milk the cows, go on errands, and go to school. There was not a child there. That afternoon I looked the old man over, and I saw he didn't care for boys. He was kinder than I thought he was, but he could not sympathize with a child. Afterwards I took a look at his wife, and I thought she was crosser than he was. I was homesick.

When a kindly old gentleman in the village nearby gave Dwight a "brand new penny" in the name of Christ, the unhappy ten-year-old felt much better.

Back at the homestead Betsey continued to eke a meager

existence from her "regular sand heap" of a farm. Dwight tells us, "She made our clothes, and wove the cloth, and spun the yarn, and darned our stockings." When they had no wood for the stove the younger children were obliged to stay in bed to keep warm. Uncle Cyrus Holton's visits were red-letter days, for he always brought a load of logs. Dwight loathed farming, and twice when he was a teen-ager he wandered off to seek greener pastures. Each time, finding no work, he returned, disillusioned.

At seventeen he had grown into a lad of five feet ten; his health was good, and his shoulders broad and sloping. Gray-eyed, with dark brown hair, D. L.—as he now pre-ferred to be called—was considered by the girls to be "tolerably good-looking."

The railroad had linked Northfield with Boston for only a few years. Now its daily invitation to "see the big city" became too strong for a restless boy. In the spring of 1854, D. L. announced to the family, "I'm tired of this! I'm not going to stay around here any longer."

When his brother George saw that D. L. was determined to walk the eighty-three miles to Boston if he could not raise the price of a one-way ticket, he gave him five dol-lars. Once more he took leave of Betsey, and as the train chugged around the bend of the Connecticut River, D. L. Moody vowed that he would make good this time.

Uncle Samuel Socrates Holton, then a well-to-do shoe tradesman of Court Street, Boston, did not exactly lay out the red carpet for his nephew. The previous Thanksgiving in Northfield the boy had asked for a job, but his brother George had warned Uncle Samuel that in no time Dwight would be wanting to run the store. D. L. soon found that

Uncle Samuel Socrates had no plans to employ an aspiring young relative in the business.

However, Samuel's brother, Uncle Lemuel, took pity on D. L. and invited him to stay at his home until he should find employment. For two days the boy searched unsuccessfully and somewhat painfully, as he was suffering from a particularly troublesome boil on his neck. After learning that his impetuous country nephew had announced his intention of walking on to New York, Uncle Lemuel persuaded Dwight to sink his pride and again ask Uncle S. S.—as Samuel Socrates was called by the family—for a job.

This time Uncle S. S. was more considerate. He gave the boy a fatherly talk which included a string of conditions for working in the store, ending with a promise from D. L. that he would not attempt to run it. Dwight accepted the offer.

After boarding in several houses, D. L. moved into a room over the shoe store, which proved to be a splendid grandstand for viewing the frequent abolitionist meetings at nearby Faneuil Hall.

It was a happy day when the boy made the acquaintance of the Young Men's Christian Association. Less than three years old, the Boston headquarters was the first in the United States, founded one week after the Canadian branch opened in Montreal.

To his mother Dwight wrote, "I am going to join the Christian Association tomorrow night. Then I shall have a place to go . . . I can have all the books I want to read free from expense. Only have to pay one dollar a year. They have a large room and the smart men of Boston lecture to them for nothing and they get up and ask questions."

As one of his conditions for employment, Uncle S. S. made D. L. attend Mount Vernon church, which by denomination was Trinitarian (orthodox Congregationalist). At home in Northfield the boy had been a Unitarian. Churchgoing had always bored D. L., so he was fortunate to have Edward Kimball as his Sunday school teacher. This man won D. L.'s devotion when, after having announced the reading from John, he quietly handed his own open Bible to the new student who was looking for the place in Genesis.

The episode greatly amused the other young men. Moody recalls. "There were a good many Harvard students . . . I saw the fellows punching one another, 'Ah, greenie from the country.' Now, you know that is just the time when you don't want to be considered green . . . I said then that if I ever got out of that scrape, I would never be caught there again.

Next Sunday D. L. was missing from class, but kindly, sensitive Kimball persuaded him to return. After all, D. L. consoled himself, he had to "stick by" the fellow who had stood by him.

To Uncle S. S., the boy's reading the Bible aloud sounded like "the chattering of a lot of blackbirds." Apologetically, when fellow churchgoers complained, Uncle S. S. put the blame for the poor reading upon the absent, hardworking Betsey. Kimball himself later declared, "I have seen few persons whose minds were spiritually darker than was his when he came into my . . . class."

At first the preaching of the pastor, Dr. Edward Norris Kirk, had little effect on D. L., who usually slept through his sermons. As for "those rich and pious" members of the congregation, D. L. detested them.

One day, spurred by a religious revival at Mount Vernon Church, Kimball set out from his lodgings at America House with a firm decision "to speak to Moody about

Christ and about his soul." D. L. was busily engaged in wrapping shoes at the back of the store when his Sunday school teacher appeared.

"I went up to him," says Kimball, "and put my hand on his shoulder and as I leaned over I put my foot upon a shoe-box. I simply told him of Christ's love for him and the love of Christ wanted in return."

It seemed that D. L. was just ready for "the light that broke upon him," for there, at once, in the back of that shoe store in Boston, he "gave himself and his life to Christ."

Of the next day, a Sunday, D. L. later wrote, "I thought the old sun shone a good deal brighter than it ever had before—I thought that it was just smiling upon me; and as I walked out upon Boston Common and heard the birds singing in the trees, I thought they were all singing a song to me. Do you know, I fell in love with the birds. I had never cared for them before. It seemed to me that I was in love with all creation. I had not a bitter feeling against any man, and I was ready to take all men to my heart."

Unfortunately, Kimball presented his protégé before the deacons too soon, although the step was necessary in order that D. L. might attain the privilege of full church member-ship. Their oral examination was a severe test for a young man so newly arrived from the country. Trembling with nervousness, he jumbled his words until they were hardly comprehensible. When asked, "Mr. Moody, what has Christ done for us all—for you—which entitles Him to our love?" D. L. lamely replied, "I don't know. I think Christ has done a good deal for us. But I don't think of anything particular as I know of."

This was not good enough for the elders of fashionable Mount Vernon Church, who promptly deferred his mem-bership. However, they did appoint two deacons to help him so that finally on May 4, 1856, he was admitted. Even so, certain members of the grown-up congregation found D. L.'s religious ardor somewhat trying, and one of "the most cultured" ladies beseeched Uncle S. S. to instruct his nephew to "hold his peace until he should become more able to edify the meetings." To his credit, Uncle S. S. refused to do so.

In the shoe store D. L. developed an uncommon flair for business. Although his fellow clerks might not appreciate his aggressive sales method of waylaying prospective customers, in the street, his sales record outdid them all.

Notwithstanding this success, he tired of working for $15 a month, out of which he sent something home to his mother, and decided to seek broader horizons. Encouraged by the example of his Uncle Calvin Holton, who the previous spring had gone West to farm, D. L. Moody, carpet bag in hand, bought a five dollar ticket and jumped on an immigrants' train for Chicago.

Three days later, weary and grimy, he was gazing for the first time upon the raw, sprawling and wonderful city. For the young man from Northfield it was a case of love at first sight. Immediately, he dashed off an enthusiastic letter to his mother, describing how the streets were built three feet above the lake, and that some who had immigrated only ten years before were now worth "from ten to fifty thousand dollars." His own ambition was to make $100,000.

"The streets are all lade out strate and broad," he continued. ". . . You can stand and look as far as the eye can reach and try to walk out of the city but it is almost impossible for you to get out of the limits of the city." Perhaps recalling Uncle S. S. and his finicky conditions of service, he added, "It is a very lively city much more so than Boston."

Uncle Calvin Holton of Des Plaines was pleased to see his nephew, helping him to obtain a position in the shoe store operated by Charles and Augustus Wiswall, both New Englanders.

The great financial panic was as yet a year away, and business was still booming. D. L. applied his own special brand of shoe sales technique to the great satisfaction of the Wiswalls. His fellow clerks wished their "unmanageable" clients upon him, and D. L. not only sold them shoes, but "never failed to send them away in good humor." Writing home, D. L. boasted, "I have made thirty dollars a week ever since I came out here." Of his employee, Charles Wiswall said later, "His personal habits made him exact and economical."

D. L. saved his money, wisely investing in land, so that only a year after arriving in Chicago his employers predicted he would one day be a millionaire. In 1857 came the crash, followed by a national panic. Moody became Wiswal's debt collector, traveling to distant parts, searching out defaulters.

Revival meetings followed in the wake of the financial distress, Chicago being no exception. Though they might forget Him in times of plenty, as usual men and women turned back to God in times of trouble.

D. L. joined Chicago's Plymouth Congregational Church, where he was not very happy. As in Boston, the moment he opened his mouth other members of the congregation complained. He records that they would "squirm their shoulders when I got up." Now it was Uncle Calvin who was asked to "shut him up" for lack of grammar.

Visiting the First Baptist Church, he met a clever thirteen-year-old girl named Emma Charlotte Revell, whom he would later remember. Sometimes D. L. visited the Presbyterian Church. On Sunday afternoons he could be found in the company of J. B. Stillson, an architect, who was a little his senior. Together they explored the vast slum areas where, according to Stillson, "We became co-workers in scattering religious reading among sailors in saloons, boarding houses and hundreds of poor families living in shanties."

This was really the beginning of D. L.'s remarkable Sunday school work for poor children. He had already been spurred by his conscience to rent five pews in his own church, which he soon filled with young men of no particular religious inclination. Now he found a small mission on North Wells Street where he asked the superintendent if he might teach. He was told he could instruct all he could get to attend the mission. On the following Sunday morning, D. L. turned up with eighteen ragamuffins, all dirty, barefooted and undernourished. He had more than doubled the mission's Sunday school roll of sixteen members! "That was the happiest Sunday I have ever known," wrote Moody. "I had found what my mission was."

The class grew so large that during the summer he taught out of doors on the shore of Lake Michigan. When winter came, he located his school in a former saloon on Michigan Street, in the heart of the sordid slum dwellings known as "the Sands." Ironically, the saloon headquarters had once been called the Mansion House.

Like the Master he sought to serve, D. L. went out among the poor, searching for converts. The gangs of ragged street boys were his chief concern. One such gang was under the dubious leadership of the much-feared "Butcher" Kilroy. It took D. L. many promises, much candy and an equal amount of courage to guide "Butcher" into the flock. He describes him as he found him: "It was a cold day in February; but the only garment (Kilroy) had was a man's old overcoat, so ragged that it had to be stitched together around his body, giving him the appearance of being sewed up in a great dirty bag. A big pair of shoes, and papers around his legs, completed his winter costume."

With "Butcher" came the gang, all fourteen of them boasting such appropriate nicknames as "Darby the Cobbler," "Rag Breeches Cadet," "Billy Buckteeth" and "Kackey Candles." "Butcher" informed his followers that they now had a new role in life. They were no longer "Kilroy's Gang" but "Moody's Bodyguard"!

Moody now rode a small pony through the dismal labyrinths of "the Sands," searching out his pupils. On Sunday morning the pony would be laden with dirty youngsters. Those who could not find room on its back held onto the stirrups, tail, or each other.

A Thanksgiving service held by Moody for his Sunday school is described by a visiting pastor:

> There were no gas fixtures in the house and he was trying to light it with a half-dozen candles; but the darkness had rather the best of it. I found him with a candle in one hand, a Bible in the other, and a child on his knee, which he was trying to teach. There were twenty-five or thirty children in all, and they were as sorry a lot of ragamuffins as could be found in Chicago.

It was understandable that as D. L.'s revival among the children grew, so would his need for larger premises. Through the intervention of former Mayor Long John Wentworth, Moody's Sunday school was given the rent-free use of a large hall which stood on the site of the former

North Market. Every Saturday night the local German Society held their dances, leaving the place in chaotic disorder. Before Moody could hold his classes, he and his friends had to clear up, but D. L. never spared himself or his friends. Nobody had a chance to come and watch, for Moody would soon delegate a job to him. The startled visitor would be bluntly ordered to mop up beer stains or retrieve cigar stubs.

The noise was terrific; only Moody could keep any semblance of order. A new teacher would be welcomed by a chorus of voices shouting, "Shine, mister, shine!" and "Morning paper!"

Then, according to one visitor, John V. Farwell, wealthy owner of a drygoods store, when Moody began to speak, the turbulent crowd of youngsters became perfectly quiet. "Moody literally held that multitude of 1,000 in his hand. His words were vivid pictures and full of emotion that tenderly touched the heart of each hearer."

When a boy came into service wearing his hat, one of Moody's Bodyguard smacked his head "with the air of one who performed a meritorious act."

To Farwell's surprise, he (Farwell) was elected Sunday school superintendent at the end of his first meeting.

Sunday school sessions often bristled with excitement, as on the day a certain boy plagued his teacher, one of the recruited friends. D. L., unable to stand the interruptions any longer, whispered in Farwell's ear, "I am going to take that boy into the police office below and whip him, and when you see me start for him have the school rise and sing the loudest hymn in the book until I return."

When D. L., his face red from this type of religious exercise, returned to the hall, he told Farwell, "It was hard work but I think we have saved him." They had. In fact, he grew up to support Moody enthusiastically in his 1878 Chicago campaign.

November 25, 1860, was a red letter day for the mission when it was honored with a visit from President-elect Abraham Lincoln. The latter was visiting Chicago to meet Vice-President Hannibal Hamblin. Farwell, who had supported Lincoln, had called at his hotel to invite him to visit the mission. Lincoln was out but Mrs. Lincoln received him kindly, promising that her husband should attend on the following Sunday afternoon.

On Sunday morning, Lincoln worshipped in St. James Episcopal Church, and during lunch he received a message that Mr. Farwell's carriage was waiting. On the way to the mission the President-elect told Farwell that he did not wish to make a speech. However, both of them had reckoned without young Mr. Moody, who simply announced, "Mr. Lincoln has come to see the school on condition that he not be asked to speak. But if he wishes to say a word before leaving, we all have our ears open."

Lincoln generously rose to the occasion. Bidding the boys listen to their teachers, he said, "I was once as poor as any boy in the school, but I am now President of the United States, and if you attend to what is taught you here, some one of you may yet be President of the United States."

When Moody left the Wiswalls' employment to become traveling salesman for C. H. Henderson's wholesale boot and shoe company, he boarded with a Mrs. Hubert Phillips, among whose other lodgers was Levi Zeigler Leiter, later to become a millionaire and father-in-law of Lord Curzon, Viceroy of India and British Foreign Secretary. Leiter always declared that had Moody stayed in the business world, in time he, too, would have become a million-aire.

In January, 1860, Moody visited Northfield, his religious zeal causing something of a local sensation. Betsey Moody's brother-in-law Zebulon Allen leaves us this on-the-spot account:

> My nephew Dwight is crazy crazy as a March hare. Came on from Chicago last week for a flying visit. I had not seen him but he drove into my yard this morning. You know how cold it was and his face was red as red flannel. Before I could say good morning he shouted "Good morning Uncle Zebulon, what are you going to do for Christ today?" Of course I was startled and finally managed to say "Come in Dwight and we will talk it over." "No I can't stop but I want you to think about it" and he turned the sleigh around and went up the hill like a streak of lightning. I tell you he is Crazy.

Back in Chicago the newspapers also called him crazy—"Crazy Moody"—but that did not prevent the same Emma Revell whom he had met in the First Baptist Church from falling in love with him. Beautiful, elegant and well-educated, she was the exact opposite to Moody. Her father, Fleming Hewitt Revell, a French Huguenot shipbuilder, had emigrated first to England, where he took an English bride, and then, in 1849, to America. His daughters Anna, Emma, Sarah and Mary had all been born in England; his son, Fleming Hewitt, Jr., in America. Mary had remained in England with her maternal aunt.

Emma was not strong like D. L., but suffered from chronic asthma and frequent headaches. She was as quiet and retiring as Moody was boisterous and loud. They were not formally engaged until she was seventeen, but this did not prevent her applying some polish to her "rough diamond."

Emma's courtship by D. L. was not a very private affair. When mission school, where she had been recruited to teach, was over for the day, he walked her home with the other girls. Eventually he startled the congregation by announcing in his usual loud voice that he could no longer accompany the other girls home because he had become engaged to Miss Emma Revell.

One day an event occurred that was to leave a deep impression upon D. L.'s life. One of his own mission teachers told him, "Well, Moody, the doctor tells me that I can't live. I have been bleeding at the lungs, and I am going home to my widowed mother to die."

D. L. asked if he were frightened, only to receive the answer, "No, sir, I am not afraid, but I am anxious for my Sabbath school. None of them are converted."

Moody thought fast. He records that, having hired a carriage, for the man was too weak to walk, "We went from house to house, visiting each scholar. And as he got out of the carriage, he would reel in his weakness across the sidewalk to the doors and call them—Martha, Mary, Julia . . ."

After ten days the teacher was able to tell Moody, "The last one of my class has yielded herself to Christ. The great vital question of their lives is settled. They have accepted my Savior. My work is done and I am going home."

Moody was a wizard with money. Since first coming to Chicago he had saved $7,000 from his shoe salesman earnings. This he gave to the poor and needy when, after "three months of the severest struggle of my life" he put aside his ambition to make $100,000, in order to become chairman of the visitation committee to sick and strangers at the Chicago

Y.M.C.A. There his noon prayer meetings were soon filled to capacity. No longer could he afford to lodge at Mrs. Hubert Phillips' house. Instead, his bed was a bench in the Y's prayer room. Although he flourished on the cheapest food he could buy, Emma gave him good meals at her home whenever she could. With his money given away, and his refusal to accept a salary from the Y.M.C.A., their prospects of marriage seemed far away.

His friend J. H. Harwood commented, "That a young man full to overflowing of animal spirits and interest in everyday life, should be able for Christ's sake to put the world completely under his feet and ask for nothing that this world had to give is not to be accounted for on any natural principle."

But on Thursday, August 28, 1862—a very hot day— Emma Revell became Mrs. D. L. Moody. The ceremony was performed in the First Baptist Church, Chicago, much to the disgust of Betsey Moody. She could not understand how her son could marry a girl born in England, and a Baptist, besides.

D. L., whose spelling was never his strong point, wrote after the ceremony about "my weding tower." Emma carefully inscribed in the Family Bible the words "D. L. Moody to Emma C. Revell; 28th August 1862."

Then Emma took the formidable Betsey to task. She wrote her unhappy mother-in-law, "It makes very little difference to what sect we belong as long as our hearts are right in the sight of God. Besides, some of Mr. Moody's warmest friends are Unitarian." Betsey was appeased and for many years afterwards watched for the regular flood of letters she received from her "favorite daughter-in-law."

With the War between the States now in full progress, Moody's services were needed not only at nearby Camp Douglas, a recruiting center, but in the front lines as well. At Fort Douglas, Moody strode from tent to tent exchanging hymnbooks for playing cards. Writing home to a brother, January 13, 1862, he notes: "I have just raised enough money to erect a chapell for the soldiers at the camp three miles from the city." This chapel, costing $2,300, was the first of its kind ever constructed for American troops.

As a member of the United States Christian Commission, D. L. visited the front nine times during the course of the war. In January, 1862, he served under fire at the Battle of Murfreesboro. Striding among the wounded, he would ask them four words, "Are you a Christian?"

At the end of hostilities he could write from experience, "Ah, our nation sowed, and how in tears and groans she had to reap!"

In 1863, by selling 40,000 shares at a quarter apiece, D. L. Moody was able to raise enough money to build his mission a permanent meeting place.

On October 24, 1864, their first child, named Emma Revell, was born to the Moodys. Like her father, she had two crooked little fingers.

Three years later, because of Emma's recurring bouts of asthma, a sea voyage was recommended for her by her doctors. With the help of friends, D. L. and Emma Moody were able to sail from New York for England, February 24, 1867, on the *City of Washington*. The baby was left in the care of Mrs. Revell so that Emma could peacefully enjoy her visit with her sister Mary in London.

Among the people D. L. was particularly anxious to

meet in England was Charles Haddon Spurgeon (1834-1892) British evangelist.

Spurgeon, three years older than Moody, had found fame in England for his preaching and printed sermons. Jolly, mostly self-taught, and somewhat plump, he was extremely popular with the masses. "Everything that I could get hold of in print that he ever said, I read," declared Moody.

Moody's first British press notice read: "Mr. D. L. Moody of Chicago, who is now in London, gives a most gratifying account of the Lord's work in different parts of America."

Arriving at Spurgeon's famed Metropolitan Tabernacle, London, built in 1861 to seat six thousand persons, Moody was bluntly told that he had to have a ticket. This was no deterrent to the former top shoe salesman. Soon he had inveigled himself an invitation inside and was listening spellbound to Spurgeon's sermon.

At a Sunday School Union meeting held May 13 in London, D. L. shocked the strait-laced with his remarks made after the vice-chairman had declared, "We are very glad to welcome our American cousin, the Reverend Mr. Moody of Chicago."

D. L. took the vice-chairman to task. "To begin with, I'm not the 'Reverend Mr. Moody' at all. I'm plain Dwight L. Moody, a Sabbath school worker. And then I'm not your American cousin. By the grace of God I'm your brother, who is interested, with you, in our Father's work for His children. And now, about this vote of thanks to the 'noble Earl [Lord Shaftesbury, the philanthropist].' I don't see why we should thank him any more than he should thank us. When at one time they offered to thank our Mr. Lincoln for presiding over a meeting in Illinois, he stopped it. He said he'd tried to do his duty, and they'd tried to do theirs. He thought it was an even turn all around."

One of the most decisive outcomes of the English adventure was Moody's meeting with youthful Harry Moorhouse, then know as the Boy Preacher. An ex-prize fighter from Yorkshire, Harry was also a reformed pickpocket. Introducing himself to Moody in Dublin, he said that he would preach for him in America. Moody, thinking him to be joking, brushed the boy off. However, a few weeks after the Moodys returned to Chicago, Harry wrote that he had arrived in New York and was en route for Chicago.

Moody was out of town upon the boy's arrival but did arrange for him to preach at his church. Returning, he asked Emma how the congregation had liked the former prize fighter.

"Oh, very much indeed," she said, "and I think you would like him too, for he proved everything he said out of the Scripture. He has preached both times from the same text, 'God so loved the world that He gave His only begotten Son.'"

Harry stayed on to become a favorite in the Moody household. He advised D. L., "Mr. Moody, you are sailing on the wrong tack. If you will change your course, and learn to preach God's words instead of your own, He will make you a great power for good."

D. L. duly responded, as his brother-in-law Fleming Revell noted. "D. L. Moody had great power before, but nothing like what he had after dear Harry Moorhouse came into our lives and changed the character of the teaching and preaching in the chapel."

From the little Englishman Mr. Moody had learned not only how to interpret the Bible for a congregation but also how to get the most out of reading it aloud. In the years to come, these lessons were to prove valuable assets for his evangelical campaigns.

Meanwhile life was happy for D. L. and his Emma, living in their new State Street house, built by the faithful Farwell as a further token of his friendship and furnished down to the bric-a-brac by friends, with a portrait of Moody by George Healy, who had painted Abraham Lincoln, in a prominent place. William Revell Moody was born March 25, 1869.

In July, 1870, D. L. attended the Y.M.C.A. International Convention where he made the acquaintance of a handsome, immaculately dressed young man named Ira David Sankey, aged twenty-nine. A revenue man for the United States Government, with a home at New Castle, Pennsylvania, Sankey was married to a beautiful, shy woman named Fanny. Until his fateful meeting with D. L. Moody, Ira Sankey's career seemed settled. In time he would receive a worthwhile pension.

Moody, who fully understood the moving power of a hymn, could not sing in any kind of harmony. His voice was described as resembling "one of the notes of the organ, sounding when it ought to be silent." When the mutton-chop-bewhiskered Sankey sang, "There is a Fountain Filled with Blood" at a prayer meeting during the convention, his fate was sealed. D. L. knew that Sankey was his man.

"Where are you from?" he demanded. "Are you married? What is your business?"

The astonished Sankey had scarcely had time to answer when he was simply told, "You will have to give that up."

Sankey stood amazed, at a loss to understand why the man told him that he would have to give up a good position. At last the singing revenue man ventured to ask, "What for?"

"To come to Chicago to help me in my work," was the firm answer.

Sankey eventually talked the matter over with his wife and did just that. Fanny Sankey, like Emma Moody, was a woman of some mettle. Most wives would have resented the price her husband had to pay in order to join forces with Moody. His entire career was literally being thrown away.

Fanny had no idea then that the names of Moody and Sankey were to become household words upon both sides of the Atlantic in the great wave of religious revivalism that would permeate the next two decades. Sankey always retired into a back room to smoke his pipe while Moody was preaching, perhaps on the theme of the Prodigal Son. At the close he would appear in time to sing, "Come Home, O Prodigal Child." Sankey's hymns stressed the most forceful points of Moody's sermons. The partnership worked out as Moody had predicted at the beginning of their association: "You see that I was right; your singing has been very helpful to all the meetings, and I am sure you ought to come to Chicago at once and give up your business."

October 8, 1871, was a Sunday that Moody would never forget. He had preached on the words of Pontius Pilate, "What then shall I do with Jesus which is called Christ?" Sankey's follow-up solo, "Today the Savior Calls," was abruptly interrupted by the din of fire trucks and pealing churchbells. Chicago was on fire.

In the holocaust that followed, the Moodys and Sankeys escaped with their lives. Emma managed to save for posterity the Healy portrait of her husband (to his personal chagrin); Moody rescued his Bible. Their children, sent with a neighbor to safety, were not reunited with them for twenty-four hours, and Emma's hair started to turn gray overnight. The fire lasted until Wednesday. When Moody, along with other survivors, viewed the wreckage, the only thing left intact in the Farwell's gift home was little Emma's toy iron stove, which was still in perfect condition.

Leaving Emma and the children with her sister Sarah, who lived on Chicago's West Side, Moody went on a preaching tour to raise funds for rebuilding his burned church and mission. At Philadelphia he stayed in John Wanamaker's mansion, and in Brooklyn he was a guest in Theodore Cuyler's church on Lafayette Avenue. He took supper with Lydia Wooster Harris, the Hudson River painter and women's rights exponent who had pensioned off her English husband Edward upon their honeymoon, finding him to be a hindrance to her work. Lydia, an expert guitarist, was soon requested by her bearded dinner guest to play a hymn. When D. L. ordered her, as he had Sankey, to "come to Chicago to help me in my work," adding that she would never be lonely again, Mrs. Harris tartly replied, "I am never less lonely than when I am alone." However, she did give D. L. a generous donation, and so did her sister Sarah Marion Combes, wife of Hiram G. Combes, executive buyer for John Wanamaker.

It was during this New York-Brooklyn visit that D. L. records, "God revealed Himself to me, and I had such an experience of His love that I had to ask Him to stay His hand . . . I was all the time tugging and carrying water. But now I have a river that carries me. . . ."

The river was Moody's revivalism.

Then began the tide of Moody evangelism that swept Britain as she had not been swept since the days of John Wesley.

"Church and state" in Victoria's domain were, according to a contemporary description, "at ease in a Zion of roast beef and port wine." Once more the timing was perfect for the harvest of souls.

Farwell did his best to persuade Moody to stay in Chicago, where, on Christmas Eve, 1871, he had opened a new tabernacle built of pinewood. But, early in 1873, while preaching in the Second Presbyterian Church, Chicago, Moody expressed an earnest desire "to get back to Great Britain and win ten thousand souls!"

A lady who preferred to be known as Aunty Cook was so bold as to inquire, "Are you going to preach to the miserable poor?"

"Yes," bellowed Moody defiantly, "And to the miserable rich too!"

John Farwell was understanding. Before Moody left America (June 7, 1873) on the *City of Paris*, he gave him a check for $500, with which the Moodys and Sankeys were able to pay for their passages. Arriving at Liverpool, they were met by Harry Moorhouse with the disturbing news that two of the men who had promised to arrange their evangelistic campaign had died, and the other was seemingly indifferent.

Undismayed, Moody remarked, "God seems to have closed the doors. We'll not open any ourselves. If He opens the door we'll go in. If He don't, we'll return to America."

God did open the door. They began their campaign in York. Lukewarm at first but gathering momentum, the preaching of Moody, augmented by Sankey's cheerful gospel singing, began to make headlines. New life was being noticeably infused into the nonconformist churches that bravely gave Moody and Sankey their local sponsorship. The *Newcastle Chronicle* spoke glowingly of the "wonderful religious phenomenon." As in his early days in Chicago, Moody, Emma relates in J. C. Pollock's *Moody*, went "to the poorest, meanest streets and told the women to come and bring their babies with them." The prosperous middle classes—the "new rich"—were well represented at his meetings. In time even the aristocracy were interested enough to attend.

A landmark in the campaign was the appearance of the famed hymn book *Sacred Songs and Solos*, from originals cut from Sankey's own scrapbook. Selling at sixpence a copy or a penny for the words only, the collection would be sung on Sunday evenings in Victorian parlors for years to come. Supplies were sold out almost as soon as they left the printing press. Even the grocers' shops stocked them.

In the fall, Moody received an invitation to preach in Edinburgh, the Athens of the North, where the Reverend John Kelman, of the Free Church of Scotland, Leith, promised to form a committee among his friends.

This was a real challenge, for Moody was well aware of his educational limitations, while the Scots were noted for their theologians among both clergy and laity. As for hymn singing, only psalms were permissible. "Edinburgh first. Then you will reach the nation," declared Kelman. Moody was still apprehensive of his reception, although Emma allayed his forebodings somewhat by calling Edinburgh the most beautiful city in the world.

The revival was off to a slow start when Moody contracted tonsillitis. Professor Alexander Simpson treated it with a newfangled throat spray. Absent for one night only, Moody was in good form at the Barclay Free Church. For seven weeks he held forth in what was to prove the most surprising campaign of his entire career. The Yankee preacher even had Scotsmen laughing in church at his anecdotes. Preferring sermons of two to three hours' duration to his half-hour ones, the Scots came for miles to hear the man who made "no attempt to awaken excitement or sensation . . . no prostrations, no sudden outbursts of rapture which we have heard in former revivals." D. L. Moody, the farm boy from Northfield, the shoe salesman from Chicago, was a celebrity at thirty-six!

Dundee and Glasgow were likewise captivated; then came Belfast in Northern Ireland. Here their hosts had a pet monkey which in the middle of supper jumped from the chandelier onto Emma's head.

When it was tactfully suggested by well-meaning friends that Moody should avoid Catholic Dublin, he casually shrugged off the warning. By refusing to attack the Catholics in his sermons Moody earned Spurgeon's displeasure. The campaign worked toward a grand climax, of which *The Times of London* wrote that it was "the most remarkable ever witnessed in Ireland."

Manchester, Sheffield, Birmingham, all in time sang Moody's praises. Now only London remained to be conquered.

The London revival began on April 9 at the Agricultural Hall, Islington, a building often used for cattle shows. Chairs for more than 15,000 persons had been provided, although actually more than 16,000 attended. *The Times* was not unfriendly, although it did not appreciate Moody's telling of Biblical incidents "as if they were good American stories picked up in Chicago." Sankey's singing was applauded. According to the *Daily Telegraph* he "might be mistaken for an Englishman anywhere." Night after night, with many conversions, the revival meetings continued. Thousands, mainly from the middle classes, crowded the Agricultural Hall.

Moody seemed to generate magnetism to the overflowing congregations, looking, as he stood there, much like General Ulysses S. Grant, from whom he had borrowed the word "campaign" to describe his own battle for souls. His very enthusiasm and vigorous appearance seemed to reach out to the crowds he sought to win. Wesley and Whitefield had both been well-educated men. In comparison, Moody was bad at spelling and cared little for the rules of grammar in his preaching. Nevertheless, his very sincerity and outgoing personality made the more educated of his listeners forget his imperfections.

Moody's admirers now included people in high places. William Ewart Gladstone, until recently prime minister of England, was proud to sit upon Moody's platform. He declared, "I thank God I have lived to see the day when He should bless His church on earth by the gift of a man able to preach the gospel of Christ as we have just heard it preached!"

Matthew Arnold replied, "Mr. Gladstone, I would give all I have if only I could believe it."

Of Gladstone, Moody commented, "Gladstone is a converted man and a true and humble Christian."

Once Gladstone said, "I wish I had your chest, Mr. Moody."

"And I wish I had your head on top of it!" replied Moody.

Lord Shaftesbury was so bold as to tell Moody that his Islington meetings attracted only the middle classes. Where were the poor or, for that matter, the rich? This resulted in the hasty erection of an enormous temporary gaslit building with a tin roof on Bow Common, where each evening at 7:30 Moody would preach to eight or nine thousand of the poor. At 9 P.M. he had left the squalor of London's East End behind him, and was firmly installed in the West End's Haymarket Theatre. Here he preached to a fashionable congregation that included such notables as the Duchess of Sutherland.

The Duchess would persuade friends and relations to accompany her, including Lady Barker, who bitterly complained, "The mixture of religious fervor and the most intense toadyism of the Duchess was horribly disgusting." However she might feel, the Duke of Sutherland thanked Moody "for all the joy and strength our dear Lord has given me through you. . . ."

Quentin Hogg, the educationist and philanthropist, and his wife, whose son Douglas was to become Lord Chancellor Hailsham, were among the earliest supporters of Moody in Britain. It was a personal triumph, if not the climax of the London campaign, when Alexandra, the beautiful Princess of Wales, attended a meeting in person.

The Dowager Countess of Gainsborough, a Lady of the Bedchamber, decided it was high time that Queen Victoria should also attend a revival, but Her Majesty thought otherwise.

Wrote the Countess:

17 Hyde Park Sq.   April 26   1875   Private

Madam—

I have been thinking Your Majesty would like once to hear these American Evangelists, who are so occupying men's minds at this time—& drawing such crowds to hear them. It would interest Your Majesty I am sure, very much and if Your Majesty wished it, might it not be?

There is the Royal Box, which Your Majesty could go to quite privately.

I have the honour to be Your Majesty's devotedly attached and faithful old servant and Subject—

F. Gainsborough.

Victoria (surely tongue in cheek) took up her pen:

Dear Fanny—

I received your letter yesterday on the subject of Moody and Sankey, 'the American Evangelists'. It would never do for *me* to go to a public place to hear them, or anything of that sort, nor, as you know, do I go to *any large public place now.*

But independently of that, though I am sure they are very good and sincere people, it is not the *sort* of religious performance which I like. This sensational style of excitement like the Revivals is not the religion which *can last,* and is not, I think, wholesome for the mind or heart, though there may be instances where it does good.

Eloquent, simple preaching, with plain practical teaching, seem to me far more likely to do *real* and *permanent* good, and this can surely be heard in all Protestant Churches, whether in the Established Church or amongst Dissenters, *if* the Ministers are thoroughly earnest.

On July 13, 1875, the last revival service was held by Moody and Sankey for that particular London campaign. At least a million and a half people had seen and heard them—a record for the days before the invention of microphones, radio, television and public relations agents.

Returning to America an international celebrity, Moody now threw his efforts into evangelizing his native land. Late in 1875 he was preaching in a disused freight depot at the corner of Tenth and Market Streets, Philadelphia, leased for the occasion by his old friend John Wanamaker. He found it necessary in the City of Brotherly Love to run special classes for alcoholics.

Said the Philadelphia *Press*, "Not a sound disturbed the strange stillness which seemed to have been produced by some mighty strength of will possessed by the very unevangelical-looking gentleman standing on the platform."

Moody treated his audience at times like children. Before proceeding to read he told the Philadelphians, "In a large hall like this, it is important that we should have silence. Let us all keep still; no one walks around and no one whispers. I would now like to read a portion of the fourth gospel of St. John."

The journalists grumbled that he spoke too fast. He had a special message for smug, regular church members during the Philadelphia campaign:

"The latter class will say, 'Oh, haven't we had a splendid meeting?' They come half an hour before anyone else and take up the best seats, and they come all the time. That isn't right. If you get a good thing, pass it round to your neighbor. What we want are the workers. If you see your neighbor weeping over his sins, send him into the inquiry room."

Cashing in on Moody's popular appeal, Philadelphia advertisers likened Moody and Sankey to their own product, "Dr. Pierce's Golden Medical Discovery" (a blood and liver remedy), saying, "Those who seek to be popular must study and be familiar with the wants of the masses."

The New York Campaign (February 7-April 19, 1876) was held in P. T. Barnum's Great Roman Hippodrome on Madison Avenue. Pierpont Morgan, the banker, was campaign treasurer, and Cornelius Vanderbilt, Jr., a private guarantor. Moody preached and Sankey sang—a magic combination.

The New York Times, which had greatly criticized Moody in the past, particularly during his British campaign, could now in all honesty say of him, ". . . the work accomplished this winter by Mr. Moody in this city for private and public morals will live."

From fall, 1876, into 1877—in spite of keen competition from the presidential election campaign in which Rutherford Birchard Hayes became nineteenth President of the United States, Moody conducted a revival in his beloved Chicago. It was sadly interrupted by the sudden death of Moody's brother Samuel, one of the twins, to whom he had always been especially attached.

Boston was next on the list to be "saved." Walt Whitman, the poet, wrote that "Boston will ere long desire him [Moody] to *git*." However, Mr. Moody stayed long enough to have his say, even though he never did succeed in preaching to Harvard's students.

The World's Columbian Exposition, May 1 to October 30, 1893, provided Moody with what he called "the opportunity of a century," and he took full advantage of it.

"Let us," said he, "open so many preaching places and present so many attractions that people from all parts of the world will come and hear the gospel!"

The Moody Bible Institute of Chicago became known in religious circles as the "West Point of Christian Work."

Significant among Moody's achievements was the founding of two schools, one for boys and the other for girls, in his native Northfield, Massachusetts. The idea for it had been his brother Samuel's. Ironically, the land needed for part of these projects he bought from the family of that same Ezra Purple who had done his best to evict Betsey Moody from her home when she was still abed with the twins.

Concerning the schools, D. L. Moody's daughter-in-law, Mrs. W. R. Moody—now well past ninety—says, "They are trying to build on the foundation he laid, which was the Bible."

As if the Northfield Schools were not enough, Moody once more turned his eyes toward the Midwest and his old love, Chicago. There must be another school there, he decided, but with a difference. This one would cater to young Christian laymen "to develop and show" what they were fitted for. Noted Moody, "A young man doesn't know until he is twenty or twenty-three what he wants to do for a profession. But if he waits until then to decide to be a minister and then goes to college and seminary, he will be fifty years old by the time he is ready to begin work; and his life is half taken out of him by that time."

Miss Emeline Dryer, a school teacher who in 1873 had resigned as head of Illinois State Normal School, was instrumental in helping Moody with his plans. Strong-willed like himself, she was not the easiest of assistants, blaming her desire for a free hand in everything to her having "once been crossed in love."

On February 5, 1887, when Moody was celebrating his fiftieth birthday, the Chicago Evangelization Society was formed "to educate, direct and maintain Christian workers as Bible readers, Teachers and Evangelists who shall teach the Gospel in Chicago and its suburbs, especially in neglected fields."

Emma complained bitterly that "Mr. Moody tells me that he spent more time in committees last winter than in ten years altogether." The formidable Miss Dryer, who for years had urged him to return to work in Chicago, for she considered him to be spending much too much time at his Northfield schools, now seemed to oppose him at every turn.

The new evangelization society was to build a Bible Institute, but in July of 1887 Moody became so discouraged by the preliminary discussions that he resigned with the statement, "I have never had my heart so set on anything as on this society, but for six months I have had to oppose some of the dearest friends I have ever had & I am tired and sick of it. I now take it that God is closing the door to me in Chicago & will open some other & will in his own way overrule it all & magnify his grace."

In the furore that followed, Mrs. Cyrus McCormick, who had supported a number of young women handpicked by Miss Dryer for future evangelical work, decided that Moody's resignation was offered because he wanted absolute control of the proposed Institute. Emma wrote her nineteen pages to say that he didn't, while Moody telegraphed the withdrawal of his resignation.

Rich men and women contributed generously to the scheme. Farwell gave $100,000; Eli Leiter and Marshall Field, $10,000 each. The tactful Mrs. McCormick gave $25,000 to Moody and an equal sum to Miss Dryer to carry on her own work without upsetting Moody. For the latter gesture he was deeply grateful. On November 9, 1889, he could happily write Will, his son, "I have no trouble with Miss Dryer. I think the storm is past & it is clear sailing just now."

The Bible Institute building was dedicated January 18, 1890. By the end of the year more than a thousand students were enrolled.

Moody was busy for the rest of his life dividing his interests between his Northfield Schools, his Bible Institute in Chicago and evangelism in general. His family life was particularly happy.

In spite of a heart ailment, Moody worked harder than ever during his campaign that ran parallel to the Chicago World's Fair in 1893. The Bible Institute's register was signed by 1,933,240 people. Moody hired Forepaugh's Circus Tent for two Sundays. Its owner, seeing in Moody a drawing card, annoyed the evangelist somewhat by advertising, "Ha! Ha! Ha! Three Big Shows! Moody in the morning. Forepaugh in the Afternoon and Evening."

Moody's happiest occasions were his visits home to the Northfield that as a boy he had been so eager to leave. The Seminary girls placed lighted oil lamps in their windows to please him, "so that all the buildings were brilliantly lighted up." He cut a conspicuous figure in his "Bumblebee" suit of yellow Donegal tweed pants with waistcoat to match and brown velveteen jacket, his old rubber boots, and "an utterly disreputable hat."

Betsy, D. L.'s mother, lived to the good age of 91, in 1896. She had finally been converted from Unitarianism.

On Friday, December 22, 1899, the last call came for Dwight Lyman Moody. To the faithful Emma he said, "Mama, you have been a good wife . . ." And then—half to himself—"No pain, no valley . . . it's bliss."

Chapter Four

RODNEY SMITH,
THE GYPSY BOY

(1860=1947)

"My mother was to be buried at the dead of night. We
were only gipsies, and the authorities would not permit
the funeral to take place in the daytime."

The death of Rodney Smith's mother had a profound effect upon his life. "I shall never be like other boys, for I
have no mother," he kept telling himself. As for Cornelius
Smith, Rodney's father, the boy records, "The wild man
in my father was broken forever. My mother's death had
wrought a moral revolution in him . . . his soul was hungry
for he knew not what, and a gnawing dissatisfaction that
nothing could appease or gratify was eating out his life."

Cornelius Smith continued to provide for his family by
the only method he knew: making clothes-pegs and tin-
ware. These the children sold from door to door as their
horse-drawn *vardo* (caravan) traveled through the East-

ern counties of England. Rodney was proud of the fact that he could sell more clothes-pegs than the others, "five or six gross in a day." He was not "bashful or backwards," which would serve him well during a busy life ahead.

Rodney's childhood ambition was to own a pair of trousers. One day his father, who "stood nearly six feet high," cut down a pair of his own for the boy to wear. They were tied around Rodney's middle with a stout piece of string. Besides keeping him warm and covered they had other uses.

> A day came when we were the guests of the Prince of Wales (later King Edward VII) at Sandringham; that is, we pitched our tents on his estate. One day I helped to catch some rabbits, and these trousers turned out to be very useful. In fact, immediately the rabbits were caught, the trousers became a pair of fur-lined garments; for I carried them home inside the trousers.

Cornelius, unable to read, could draw no comfort from his Bible. One day, meeting up with the caravans of his brothers Woodlock and Bartholomew, he spoke of his "great burden," confessing simply, "I do not know how to be good." His brothers agreed to accompany him to "God's house" in search of knowledge. This proved to be the Primitive Methodist Chapel in Fitzroy Street, Cambridge. Cornelius left "that house of prayer still a convicted sinner, but not a converted one."

The next step—and for a gypsy a desperate one—was to forsake his tribal camping grounds in Epping Forest for a waste spot close to Henry Varley's Chapel at Shepherd's Bush, London. There he sold the horse, implying that he would not move his caravan until he had "found the way to God."

Cornelius was successful in his quest. Before returning to Epping Forest he sold his fiddle, insisting that it had led him "into drink, and sin, and vice, and bad company." Afterward, he preached an impromptu sermon to the men who purchased it.

"Lord, save my Rodney!"

When Cornelius (as he termed it) "prayed" his other children, Emily, Lovinia and Ezekiel, into the church, Rodney, still too full of mischief, was "not quite ready." Among other things, he had eaten his Uncle Bartholomew's plum pudding and sold a town dweller a nest of baby sparrows under the alias of baby linnets! In time, however, his "wickedness abated" so that he could follow the example of the other members of his family. He recorded in his autobiography, "The date of my conversion was the 17th of November, 1876."

About this time came a desire to learn to read and write. As the caravan traveled through the countryside Rodney would inquire from passers-by the words painted on wayside signs. Eventually he obtained copies of the Bible, an English dictionary and a Bible concordance. These the youngster liked to carry under his arm, not caring how much his brother and sisters ridiculed him for doing so. Word by word he tried to teach himself to read. As his vocabulary grew, he began to fancy himself a minister. "One Sunday," he says, "I entered a turnip field and preached most eloquently to the turnips." Now, as he walked with his basket of clothes-pegs and cake tins, Rodney sang snatches of hymns he had learned from his uncles. People called him "the singing gypsy boy."

As he approached his seventeenth birthday, his longing to become a preacher became almost an obsession. He says:

One Sunday morning I rose with the determination to undertake something in that line. I arrayed myself in my Sunday best, consisting of a small brown beaver hat, my velvet jacket with white pearl buttons, a vest with the same adornments, a pair of corduroys, and a yellow handkerchief with a dash of red in it round my neck.

Then, standing in front of his father's caravan, he sang until a crowd on their way to worship paused to listen. With his good looks and black wavy hair so characteristic of the true Romany he introduced himself "naturally as the flowers do." His preaching then, as later, was straightforward and simple. "I told the people how I had found the Saviour, what my life and desires were, and that I loved Jesus and wanted everybody else to love Him too."

That same year he met William Booth, later General Booth (1820-1912), organizer and commander of the Salvation Army. At that time Cornelius wanted to send Rodney to the Reverend Charles Spurgeon's pastors' college, but Booth, realizing the boy's potentialities, took him under his own wing. After a gospel meeting at which Rodney had sung a hymn entitled, "Happy, Ever Happy," Booth asked him, "Will you leave your gypsy home, your father, sisters and brother, and come to me to be an evangelist in the Christian Mission?" At that time Rodney did not even know the meaning of the word "evangelist," but believing it to be something good, promised to do as Booth asked.

"If I am going to be a preacher, I shall have to dress like a preacher," he decided. The next day he discarded the characteristic brightly colored gypsy neckerchief and set out to buy a frock-coat, vest and pair of striped trousers. Also, for half a crown, he obtained a box in which to carry his "preaching requirements," with a piece of clothesline to secure it.

When he left his father's caravan to become a preacher, his brothers and sisters dubbed him a *Romany Rye* (gypsy gentleman) and a *Boro Rashie* (great preacher). Two cousins carried the all-important box, practically empty, as Rodney was wearing all his finery. "I could have carried all that I had in a brown paper parcel, but the dignity of the occasion demanded a box, and (they) forbade me to carry it myself."

That night, sleeping in a room for the first time in his entire life, Rodney felt as if he were suffocating, and longed for his caravan. As for the bed, he wondered if it would hold him.

Rodney was the thirty-sixth missionary at the Christian Mission which he joined June 25, 1877. He still could not read properly, and conducting a meeting singlehanded was rather an ordeal.

"The plan I adopted was this—I went on reading slowly and carefully until I saw a long word coming into sight. Then I stopped and made some comments, after the comments I began to read again, but took care to begin on the other side of the long word. I used to struggle night after night in my lodgings over the hard words and names in the Bible."

In time perseverance brought its own reward when William Booth sent Rodney to "preach the gospel" in St. Hilda's Hall, Whitby, where his singing especially attracted the fishermen and their wives, making him a favorite in the town.

Among his converts was Annie E. Pennock, whose father was a captain in the mercantile marine. Unfortunately, Booth did not approve of a "sweethearting" missioner, and the emotional attachment that developed resulted in Rodney's transfer to another town. However, after he had been promoted to captain's rank in Devonport (the Christian Mission having become generally known as the Salvation Army), Rodney proudly traveled back to Whitby and married his patient Annie on December 17, 1879.

At Newcastle-on-Tyne, on the last day of 1880, their first child, a son, was born. They named him Albany Rodney. Captain Rodney now had an income of thirty-three shillings a week plus a free house. He felt like a king.

His first charge following his marriage was at Chatham, a difficult station. The sailors based there took an aversion to his preaching, while "the civilian population did not help us, but simply looked on, enjoying the fun, while we were being pelted and otherwise molested." Annie's encouragement was a great help in this trying situation. "I do not think I shall ever know in this world how much of my success is due to my wife," he once said.

The family grew. Alfred Hanley was born August 5, 1882, and Rhoda Zilla, February 1, 1884. During D. L. Moody's famed 1881 campaign, Rodney Smith joined the American evangelist's audience.

While working in a Salvation Army station at Hull— perhaps named literally the "Ice House"—Rodney Smith made many converts. One of the most celebrated of them was "Happy Patty," a soiled dove who, after hearing him preach, "stripped off her old filthy rags and jumped into the fountain filled with blood." Her timely conversion drew "many weather-beaten seamen" into the fold.

In 1882 "Gypsy" Smith (the name that was to make him famous) severed his connection with the Salvation Army to become a full-time evangelist in his own right. At Hanley in the Potteries, Staffordshire, where he was already well known, his first testimonial meetings were followed by popular demonstrations. Gypsy was carried home shoulder high to the accompaniment of a brass band!

A number of supporters, led by a Methodist mayor and an Anglican vicar, were so impressed with the sincerity of the young man that they formed their own committee to promote his work. The Reverend M. Baxter, editor of the *Christian Herald*, played a leading role, and the Imperial Circus, which could seat 4,000 people, was hired for a period of three months to accommodate Gypsy Smith's services.

A prayer meeting for three hundred people, preceding the main evangelical meeting, was customarily held in a disused circus dressing room over the stables. One Sunday evening in October, 1882, a near-tragedy occurred when the overstrained floor suddenly gave way. Gypsy Smith crashed into the void below, along with his praying converts. Seventy-five people were injured, but, strangely enough, the main congregation did not panic. Gypsy, nerves on edge, managed to get through the service that night, although there was one more fright when the lights failed, plunging the circus into pitch darkness. If a mining agent had not had the presence of mind to start singing a hymn, which calmed other members of the congregation, many people might well have been trampled to death.

Rodney Smith found time in his busy life to study the Reverend Charles Finney's *Lectures on Revivals*, and "something of Spurgeon and of John Wesley." He could now read well enough to appreciate Scott, Dickens, Thackeray, Tennyson—and even Byron and George Eliot. In 1883, he made his first trip abroad, visiting Sweden, where he had the opportunity of seeing the King.

His reputation as an evangelist was growing. When he

addressed the fall session of the Congregational Union of England and Wales at Hanley by invitation from the platform (having been denied the courtesy of a written invitation because he was not an ordained minister), the *Christian Herald* gave a favorable picture of him:

> When the young man rose, presenting a dark but not swarthy countenance, there was nothing, save a flash of fire in his black eyes as he gazed around upon the assembly, that would have indicated that he came of a gipsy tribe, or that he was anything different from an ordinary youth of the middle class. He certainly had never stood up in such an assembly before. His manly tone, his handsome presence, his eloquence, and his earnestness procured him a flattering reception from the assembly.

"The young gipsy's speech is as correct as his singing," the *Christian Herald* writer also noted. Rodney's self-education, encouraged by his wife, was paying rich dividends.

For the next few years he conducted gospel missions in various parts of the country until at last, because of the generosity of B. F. Byron, a cotton spinner and woolen manufacturer, Gypsy Smith was able to fulfill a long-time ambition. On January 19, 1889, he sailed on the steamship *Umbria* for a visit to America. As the ship rolled in the dock, a terrified gypsy uncle, who had traveled a hundred miles to see him off, cried out to Rodney's wife, "Annie, my dear, I shall never see him again."

Landing in New York on a wet Sunday morning, "not knowing, to the best of my belief, a single soul on the whole of the vast continent," Rodney checked in at the Astor Hotel. "Mr. Byron," he said, "had advised me to go to a good hotel." The next day, he appeared at the New York Methodist Episcopal Ministers' Meeting with a letter of introduction from a clergyman in England. Encouraged by the ministers' friendliness, he called at the offices of the *Christian Advocate*. The publication's editor, equally impressed, introduced him to the Nostrand Avenue Methodist Church, Brooklyn, where he was engaged to conduct a three-week revival.

Before the first meeting, Ira D. Sankey took him for a drive, and Rodney asked if Sankey remembered having driven out to a gypsy encampment in Epping Forest during the famous D. L. Moody revival. Sankey did, even recalling the gypsy boys—of whom Rodney had been one—who stood by the wheel of the trap he was driving.

Sankey, an immaculate dresser, had one word of advice for the gypsy evangelist.

"Brother Smith," he inquired, "why do you not wear a white tie?"

"I really do not know," was the reply.

"Well, Brother Smith," said Sankey, "I guess you would do well to buy some tonight, and wear one tomorrow."

Gypsy Smith followed his advice.

After a successful mission in Brooklyn, Rodney made a grand preaching tour of America. In a Philadelphia church, he was surprised when the minister suddenly shouted, "Go up into the choir and convert the organist!" The only sound uttered in the silence that followed was a loud "Uumph!" from the sinner in question.

In Cincinnati he visited a gypsy encampment. A local newspaper described the unusual event:

> There was a striking contrast between this civilized Romany Rye and the untamed ones that soon gathered round him. He was attired in a three-button cutaway coat and black and gray-striped pantaloons, and a white tie

peeped out from under a turned-down collar. Surrounding him was a motley gathering of men, women, and children. All gazed upon him with great curiosity, but he soon relieved them, and each eagerly tried to talk to him. The young men wore rather shabby attire, with the never absent colored handkerchief about their necks. They had but little to say, but one middle-aged, stoutly-built man, as fine a type of the gipsy as mortal man ever looked upon, was unusually friendly.

Another Cincinnati journalist quipped somewhat unkindly, "Gypsy Smith speaks as if composing cable dispatched at a cost of a dollar a word for transmission."

At Rodney's own request he took time off to visit the Germantown, Pennsylvania, home of Tom Paine, author of *The Age of Reason.* He was delighted to find that Paine's house had become a young ladies' college where "every morning, in the room which the infidel writer used for study, a meeting for prayer and study of the Bible was held." With a sense of keen satisfaction Rodney Smith noted, "That is how Christianity revenged itself on Tom Paine in Germantown!"

He was also introduced to the mother of Charles Stewart Parnell, the Irish Nationalist leader, who impatiently demanded, upon being confronted by Rodney and two ministers, "Which is the one from England?" Rodney found her to be both "sweet and gracious."

Of church life in America, Smith noted later, "You will see more handshaking after one service in America than after tea in this country. In England, when the benediction is pronounced, we rush for the door; in America they rush for one another.

"They have beautiful churches, beautifully furnished.

The floors are laid with Brussels carpets—no shabby strips of coconut matting in the aisles of American churches.

"The Americans, in short, have caught the spirit of the age. They believe in adaptation, and they believe that the Church ought to have the best of everything."

His only complaint was a common one voiced even today by English visitors. "They do stew you in their rooms in America!"

Gypsy Smith made several other evangelical safaris to America. In 1891, he welcomed a venturesome gypsy and his wife who had pitched their tents "a little outside Brooklyn" in order to hear him preach.

He marveled at "the entire absence of drink from the tables of the houses" that he visited. On his third visit he was particularly popular at the camp meetings at Ocean Grove, New Jersey, a favorite summer resort for American ministers and their families. There he met the famous colored preacher Amanda Smith, who would call out in the middle of his sermons, "That's hit the bull's-eye, Brother Smith. Hit it again!"

Gypsy Smith's American revivals were usually conducted under the auspices of Methodist Episcopal Churches. However, one of his most successful revivals—"a really united campaign," he called it—was held at Yonkers, New York, where all the ministers with the exception of the local Protestant Episcopal Church supported him.

This was one of the happiest periods of the Smiths' lives. Hundreds of people of all ages passed through the inquiry room, and rich and poor welcomed the evangelists into their homes. Among the attenders at the prayer meetings were three little old ladies who, when invited into the inquiry room at the close of a service, declared with one voice, "Oh, no, we could not go there. We could not think of it!"

"Are you a Christian?" Gypsy Smith asked of the one nearest him.

"No, sir," replied the little old lady. "I'm an Episcopalian."

The Yonkers Gleaner described Rodney as "a notable evangelist, notable for what he is, as a warm-hearted, frank, honest, effective preacher."

New York society ladies, charmed by the handsome, curly-haired gypsy and his pleasant, well-spoken wife, opened their mansions for drawing room meetings. Attenders at one such gathering, among nearly two hundred ladies, were Mrs. John D. Rockefeller, a devout supporter; Mrs. Russel Sage; and young Mrs. Joseph Botsford Whitney, a fighter for women's rights from Brooklyn Heights. Rodney Smith, the Gypsy Boy, had progressed a long way from his father's caravan in Epping Forest.

At Denver, Colorado, Mrs. Smith, who was suffering from bronchitis, was cured at once when they reached the city, while her husband's voice was so affected that he could "speak all right" but "could not sing."

Smith preached to large crowds nightly for a month, recording on one occasion that "five hundred people knelt at the Communion rail as penitents, one of whom was a Chinaman."

Denver was more generous to the Smiths than any other city in America, even paying their traveling expenses, which amounted to fifty pounds, a sizeable sum in those days.

Smith preached in Glasgow, Scotland, from September, 1893, to January, 1894, and the revival crowds were so large that Dr. George Reith, pastor of the Free College

Church in that city, commented in his church magazine: "We have seen nothing like it since the visit of Messrs. Moody and Sankey in 1874. The speaking was remarkable." The *North British Daily Mail* described the meetings as "a Glasgow Pentecost." In 1894, Smith conducted revivals in Australia. He was a bad sailor and the five weeks on the water he describes as "dreary" ones. On the occasion of his fifth visit to America in 1896, a large placard at the People's Temple announced him as GYPSY SMITH, THE GREATEST EVANGELIST IN THE WORLD.

Even D. L. Moody, himself a Yankee, had a hard time trying to convert intellectual Boston, but Rodney Smith was described in the press of that city as "a spiritual phenomenon, an intellectual prodigy, and a musical and oratorical paragon."

Smith's greatest American triumph came when he was presented to President Grover Cleveland at the White House.

Even Queen Victoria, who had refused to attend a Moody and Sankey revival, wrote him a gracious letter commending his evangelistic work.

His obvious simplicity, sincerity, eloquence of speech and quiet, disciplined life appealed to rich and poor in both countries. The Reverend George D. Low of the Fountain Bridge Free Church, Edinburgh, summed up the public impression of Smith in the *British Weekly* of June 23, 1892:

> Gipsy Smith is a born orator with great dramatic fire, of singular intensity of spirit. His voice is tuneful and flexible, and lends itself readily to the expression of every mood of mind and every form of discourse. He is specially effective when he illustrates and illuminates some point, or some Gospel truth, by an incident simple, tender, pathetic, from his old gipsy life, to which he frequently alludes as

one proud of his origin. His addresses are Scriptural, as might be expected from one who is an unwearied and resolute student of the Bible. In manner he is simple, unaffected, gentlemanly, and I can speak the more confidently regarding this as he lived under my roof while in Edinburgh, and gained the esteem and affection of every member of my household by his sunny, gracious personality. His singing, which is of great purity and excellence, adds greatly to his power.

During the last mission he was to conduct in the nineteenth century Rodney found himself at Luton, close to Baldock, where his mother had died of smallpox and been buried at dead of night because "she was only a gypsy." During this revival, the Mayor of Luton himself made a point of erecting a stone over the lonely, unmarked grave.

The text upon it testified to the work of her famous son who died at sea long afterward, on August 4, 1947, at the age of 87, once more on his way to America:

And God hath made of one blood all nations of men.

Chapter Five

THE BALLPLAYER

Billy Sunday

(1862-1935)

"I was bred and born, not in old Kentucky, (although my grandfather was a Kentuckian), but in old Iowa. I am a rube of the rubes, I am a hayseed of the hayseeds, and the malodors of the barnyard are on me yet, and it beats Pinaud and Colgate, too. I have greased my hair with goose grease and blacked my boots with stove blacking. I have wiped my old proboscis with a gunny-sack towel; I have drunk coffee out of my saucer, and I have eaten with my knife. I have said 'Done it' when I should have said 'did it,' and I 'Have saw' when I should 'Have seen,' and I expect to go to Heaven just the same. I have crept and crawled out from the university of poverty and hard knocks, and have taken postgraduate courses."

Born on November 19, 1862, in a log cabin near Ames, Iowa, William Ashley Sunday was named by the father he never saw. William Sunday, senior, the bricklayer son

of immigrant German parents named Sonntag, had en-
listed as a private with the Union Army on August 14,
1862. The following December 23 he died of pneumonia
at Camp Patterson, Missouri. Mary Jane Corey, a descendant of that same Sir Francis Drake who had scattered the
Spanish Armada, was left with three young sons to fend
for. Albert was four and Edward two.

After six lean years she remarried a shiftless man named
Heizer who fathered Elizabeth (Libbie) and Leroy. Dur-
ing the depression of 1874, Heizer casually disappeared.
With five instead of three children, the hapless Mary
Jane returned to her father's home.

Billy, hating his stepfather, had earlier moved in with
Martin (Squire) Corey, his grandfather. A kind-hearted
man of many practical talents, Squire was the second cousin
and childhood friend of General Ulysses S. Grant.

The child Billy had been much attached to his grand-
mother and after her death he was found, one wintry night,
lying across her grave. Half frozen, he was gently carried
home by "Squire" Corey.

Tragedy continued to plague Billy's mother when Albert was kicked in the head by a horse. Suffering from a
damaged brain, he had to be put in an asylum. As if this
were not enough, Libbie's dress caught alight when she
was helping with a bonfire, and she was burned to death.
In 1874 Edward and Billy were sent to the Soldiers'
Orphan Home at Glenwood, Iowa; and later, to another in
Davenport.

The boys found the Davenport home strictly disciplined. Any inmate who tried to run away was forced to
march around the cinder track in front of the main building eight hours a day for a week, with brief meal breaks.
Whippings and prayers were the order of the day. Clean-

liness was literally considered next to godliness, and Billy never forgot this early training. For the rest of his life, he was noted for his neatness.

Although he was made to learn many Bible verses by heart, Billy's interest as a boy was strictly athletic. A contemporary describes him as "fleet of foot, lithe of carriage, capable of orderly coordination of ligaments and muscles, and these things made him what sportsmen call a natural athlete." It was at the orphanage that Billy first proved his ability as a runner.

When Edward reached the age of sixteen he was required to leave the home, and his younger brother asked to be released, too. Back at "Squire" Corey's, Billy found farm chores distasteful, just as D. L. Moody had done. When his grandfather wrongfully blamed him for some small mistake, the boy borrowed a horse and rode to Nevada, Iowa, eight miles away. Then fourteen years old, he found work in a hotel, but lost his job a few months later when he went back to visit his mother and stayed a day longer than the two-day vacation allotted. This was a blessing in disguise, for his next employers were Colonel John Scott, a former lieutenant-governor of Iowa, and his sympathetic wife. Billy worked at their stable as errand boy.

Admiring his industry, the Scotts sent Billy to high school for the next four years. Besides giving him a good home, they provided eight dollars a month for pocket money. Appointed school janitor for the last two years, Billy received his schoolbooks free.

He was unable to attend graduation ceremonies for a valid reason. Having acquired local fame as a runner and athlete, he was invited by the Marshalltown Fire Brigade to join their team in the yearly fire-fighting tournament, which was held on his graduation day. At that time, membership in a fire-fighting company carried much prestige.

Besides being a fireman, after moving to Marshalltown Billy earned extra money working for an undertaker. He also took up baseball when his extraordinary base running became the talk of the town. In 1883 his team successfully carried off the state championship.

At this time Billy Sunday was brought to the attention of Adrian C. (Pop) Anson, manager of the Chicago Whitestockings, a professional team owned by A. G. Spalding, which fell into the big-league category. Pop's Aunt Emily was one of Billy's local Marshalltown Diamond fans.

After seeing Billy in action, Anson persuaded him to forsake firefighting and undertaking for the more remunerative profession of baseball. His new salary was sixty dollars a month. Billy arrived in the Windy City with only a dollar in change, and the other Whitestockings made such fun of the country boy's six-dollar sage-green suit that he won their respect only after beating, barefooted, their fastest athlete.

In time, Billy gained the reputation of becoming "an excellent outfielder" and the Whitestockings' fastest runner. According to Sunday, during his eight years in baseball (1883-1891) he made two records not beaten for many years. After a standing start, he once rounded the bases in fourteen seconds; while in one season he managed to steal ninety-five bases. In 1915 Ty Cobb broke this last record by one base.

"But there were better hitters," Billy later admitted. "One year with the White Stockings I had an average of .359, and I was only fourteenth in the National League when Cap Anson led it with an average of .420."

Anson called his Aunt Emily's discovery the team's best player "on his feet" but "a poor batter."

It was in Chicago that Billy first met Helen A. Thompson, known to her family as Nell, who had been "converted" at the early age of fourteen. Nell's parents were of Scottish background. Her father, William Thompson, was a Chicago dairyman and ice cream manufacturer who, during the Civil War, had been wounded at the Battle of Shiloh. The entire family were Presbyterians.

By luck, Nell's brother, William Thompson, Jr., was bat boy and mascot for the Whitestockings, which provided an excuse for their frequent meetings. Although Billy's mother was a Methodist, Billy joined Jefferson Park Presbyterian Church, the scene of Nell's labors with the Christian Endeavor Society. Nell's father did not approve of his "religious" daughter's keeping company with a professional ballplayer, so Billy and Nell had to devise new ways of seeing one another. Nell swept the family steps several times a day at prearranged times when Billy would be passing.

Mr. Thompson might never have consented to a serious courtship but for a great change that took place in Billy Sunday's life. One day in 1886 he was converted.

It was a sudden, unpremeditated conversion. In years to come Billy would tell vast congregations about it.

> . . . I walked down a street in Chicago in company with some ball players who were famous in this world—some of them are dead now—and we went into a saloon. It was Sunday afternoon and we got tanked up and then went and sat down on a corner. I never go by that street without thanking God for saving me. It was a vacant lot at that time. We sat down on a curbing. Across the street a company of men and women were playing on instru-

ments—horns, flutes, and slide trombones—and the others
were singing the gospel hymns that I used to hear my
mother sing back in the log cabin in Iowa and back in
the old church where I used to go to Sunday School.
. . . I arose and said to the boys, "I'm through. I am going
to Jesus Christ. We've come to the parting of the ways,"
and I turned my back on them. Some of them laughed,
and some of them mocked me; one of them gave me encouragement; others never said a word.

Billy immediately renounced swearing, drinking, gam-
bling and theatergoing. Now, instead of playing baseball
on Sundays, he could be found speaking at the Y.M.C.A.
He called his talk "Earnestness in Christian Life."

Striving to please Nell and her parents, during the winter
of 1887-88 Billy enrolled at Evanston Academy, the pre-
paratory school for Northwestern University. There, in
return for his studies, he coached the college baseball team.
His diction improved enormously. On September 5, 1888,
Billy and Nell were married.

The next winter, he studied the Bible at the Chicago
Y.M.C.A., where he felt that he was "definitely called to
enter Christian work." Since he had signed a three-year
contract with the Philadelphia team, getting his release
presented no small problem.

Said Billy, "I made it a matter of most earnest prayer,
and even went so far as to make a proposition, saying,
'Lord, if I don't get my release by March 25th, I will take
that as assurance You want me to continue to play ball;
if I get it before that date I will accept that as evidence
You want me to quit playing ball and go into Christian
work.' "

Billy was released on March 17. However, this was not

the end of the matter, for he immediately received a tempting offer of $500 a month to play for the Cincinnati team.

With his wife, his new baby daughter and his mentally retarded brother to support (Billy's mother had gone to the altar for the third time and needed no help), the decision as to whether to forsake baseball for $33.33 a month at the Y.M.C.A. was one requiring the wisdom of a Solomon. Fortunately, the question was quickly settled by Nell, who said, "There is nothing to consider. You promised God to quit."

Billy's schedule at the Y.M.C.A. proved a full one, entailing a fourteen-hour working day. L. W. Messer, the general secretary, said, "We never had a man on our staff who was more consecrated, more deeply spiritual, more self-sacrificing. He was especially strong in his personal effort among men who were strongly tempted and among those who had fallen by the way."

Billy was required to preach on street corners, find speakers for the meetings in Farwell Hall, hand out religious literature in saloons, conduct prayer meetings and save derelicts. His salary was increased to $1,200 the second year, and $1,500 the third, but because of the depression of 1893 he did not always get it.

When the hymn-writer P. P. Bilhorn suggested Billy to the Reverend Dr. J. Wilbur Chapman, popular evangelist, as an assistant, the latter's offer of $40 a week was gratefully accepted.

Billy became Chapman's "advance guard." It was his job to see that all preparations were made beforehand by the community where Chapman would preach. Among his duties was that of ensuring that enough contributions had been made to pay for the hall rental and newspaper notices. He was responsible for training the committee of sponsoring townsfolk. When the revival actually got under way, Billy Sunday was master of ceremonies while Chapman did the actual preaching. Once Billy spotted former President Benjamin Harrison in the audience and rallied him onto the platform. Even then Billy could be very persuasive.

Suddenly, in December, 1895, Chapman decided to become pastor of Bethany Church, Philadelphia, founded by John Wanamaker. Billy was stunned by Chapman's telegram, which came during the Christmas festivities when he was home with Nell in Chicago. The Sundays wondered whether Billy should return to professional baseball, but such a step proved unnecessary when an unexpected invitation came from a number of ministers in Garner, Iowa, soliciting his services to lead a revival.

With no sermons prepared other than his Y.M.C.A. talk "Earnestness in Christian Life," Billy was uncertain what to do. He had no money for publicity and had never before conducted a revival on his own. Nevertheless, with Nell's encouragement, he accepted the challenge.

Garner, boasting a population of approximately one thousand, was situated in Iowa's corn belt. The town's three Protestant churches had temporarily united for the campaign. As Billy had no gospel singer—a "drawing-card" used by all evangelists since D. L. Moody—a choir of sorts was mustered, with Billy, who confessed that he "did not know a note from a horsefly," doing his best to lead it.

Said the *Hancock Signal* of the budding evangelist, "This must be 'Billy' Sunday who used to play ball for Anson with the Chicago Whitestockings. Billy is as true a Christian gentleman as he was a rattling ball player, and that is saying a good deal."

At the conclusion of the week's meetings there were one

hundred conversions and a "love-offering" for Billy amounting to just $68.

But this was only the beginning. Billy was still in Garner when he was asked to campaign in another part of the State, at Sigourney. This time the advance newspaper notice inserted by the Baptist, Christian, Presbyterian and Methodist churches announced him as the "Reverend" William Sunday, not being aware that he was as yet unordained to a regular ministry.

They also found him a choir leader with the endearing name of Joseph E. Van Winkle. The two were a great success. A local newspaper editor paid Billy the supreme evangelical compliment: "His sermons are similar to those of Mr. Moody."

During the next five years, Billy conducted about sixty similar campaigns in the Iowa corn belt. At this time his approach was no different from that traditionally prescribed by "Mr. Moody." In 1896 he was still refusing to preach on Sunday, requiring the pastors of his sponsoring churches to fill their own individual pulpits on that day.

The spectacle of a famous young baseball star giving up his career for Christ had intrigued the newspapers from the start. He was even fêted in poems like this one, from the Atlantic (Iowa) *Semi-Weekly Telegraph:*

> Four weeks he's been here preaching,
>   I tell you it was grand;
> They say that more than twenty score
>   On the Lord's side took their stand.

Billy Sunday was now receiving month-long engagements instead of the meager one week he was allowed in the beginning.

However, revivals in small towns had their headaches.

Often the churches were too small to hold capacity crowds and Billy had to use tents. In the beginning he had to erect them and take care of them himself.

In 1900 he was in a position to hire his own permanent gospel singer, Fred Fischer, who stayed with him for ten years. Fred was the type of dream man most attractive to women of the time. His good looks, huge physique and walrus mustache were offset to perfection by the *pièce de résistance*, his pince-nez.

Nell Sunday took charge of her husband's business arrangements. The births of George, Paul and William further increased the family. In order to accompany Billy she left the children with her parents.

In 1908 the Chicago Presbytery ordained Billy Sunday a minister, and Dr. Chapman preached the sermon. On June 13, 1912, Dr. R. M. Russell, president of Westminster College, New Wilmington, Pennsylvania, conferred upon him an honorary degree of Doctor of Divinity.

The revivals up to 1906 had been mainly confined to small towns in Iowa, Wisconsin, Nebraska, Missouri, Illinois, Minnesota and Indiana, but now the more conservative of the clergy in these states were beginning to criticize him. Billy no longer insisted that they fill their own pulpits on Sundays, but now demanded that all sponsoring churches should discontinue their regular services during his stay. "Infidelity," he insisted, "is rampant, and rank unbelief is preached from many a pulpit."

The ministers in turn pointed out that Billy Sunday revival meetings were in danger of becoming "popular entertainment" instead of "sacred gatherings." Sometimes Billy even used a rented twelve-piece orchestra. The truth was that revivals themselves were changing. Businessmen, recognizing him as "an up-to-date man," fit for the new century, rallied to his platform.

In 1905, when Billy was preaching in Salida, Colorado, a snowstorm broke the center poles of his tent and tore it to ribbons, causing him to substitute a wooden "tabernacle" for future campaigns.

Tabernacles were plain, temporary structures built of wood, with tarpaper roofs, containing hundreds of pine benches for the congregation. A speaker's platform was the most prominent feature. The walls were so arranged that in the event of fire whole sections could be pushed out for use as emergency exits.

When Billy Sunday had used his first tabernacle at Perry, Iowa, back in 1901, the feet of the congregation had made such a clatter on the wooden floor that Billy ordered sawdust to be thrown down to deaden the sound. The local firemen raised objections because of the pot-belly stoves, but Billy threw hot coals on the floor to prove that sawdust was not inflammable.

As Sunday's fame spread, the business side of the enterprise improved. Ministers in small towns could not always raise the necessary expense money to see a revival through. In 1904, at Keokuk, Billy stipulated that ministers should receive advance pledges amounting to $2,000 from members of their churches, not to be used unless the free will offerings at the actual revival fell short of the required sum for covering expenses.

Billy's teaching technique was unique. When endeavoring to stress a point he could use ridicule and mimicry to perfection. Now he attempted to improve the moral life of every community he visited as a preacher. The saloonkeepers dreaded his coming, for Billy hated liquor and everybody connected with it.

He had a simple, grass-roots solution for everything. Here are some typical examples of his two-fisted preaching style:

There isn't an angel in heaven who wouldn't be tickled to death to come down to earth and be honored with motherhood.

No wonder the men go to their clubs, with these women bumming around bridge parties, gadding and fondling pet dogs. No man wants to play second fiddle to a bowlegged bull pup. You may bet your sweet life I wouldn't.

I like good old Anglo-Saxon words. They mean more and have more power behind them. If I should come here and say you were prevaricators and evaders of the truth instead of calling you the liars that some of you are, it would make no more impression than water on a duck's back. Slang gets the thing in a nutshell and makes it easy for the people to understand. Preachers would get along much better if they used words of a plainer type so that the ordinary class would know what they are talking about.

You mothers are fools to force your daughters to marry some old lobster simply because he has money, and when he dies your girl will be able to ride in a buzz wagon instead of hot-footing it. You're fools!

Christ says, "What God hath joined together let no man put asunder." The world says, "We'll divorce you and then we'll marry some other woman and we won't sin!" *You lie!*

The only scriptural excuse for divorce is adultery. When it comes to the divorce question, I'm a Roman Catholic from the top of my head to the soles of my feet.

As the years passed, Billy Sunday became a figure of national importance. His services as an evangelist were booked, sometimes years in advance, by the largest cities in the nation. "Somewhere during the period," says the *New York Times*, "Billy Sunday had been transformed from the revivalist of dignity, carrying on the dignified tradition of Moody, to the acrobatic dervish of evangelism."

Billy's fundamentalist theology, well spiced with patriotic Americanism, gained him a tremendous following among the crowds. When criticized for the "man-made look" of his form of revivalism, he answered with the words of Charles Grandison Finney (1792-1875), the frontier revivalist: "God Almighty may use any method or means or individual that he pleases in order to promote a revival."

Fischer, now dated like his pince-nez, was replaced in 1910 by Homer Alvin Rodeheaver, who fitted to perfection the role of twentieth-century chorister. Born in Cinco Hollow, Ohio, in 1880, he had spent his childhood in Jellico, Tennessee, where his father had a sawmill. As a boy he learned to play the cornet, later at Ohio Wesleyan College turning his attention to the trombone. His personal charm could warm up any audience for the climatic appearance of Billy Sunday—sometimes called in the contemporary press "God's mouthpiece."

Rodeheaver, popularly known as Rody, could perform tricks like a magician. Sometimes he made weird, irreligious sounds on his trombone. He was described as "one of the greatest adjuncts a revivalist ever had" and "as appealing a figure on the platform as [William Jennings] Bryan." His baritone voice was good, and his smile was the delight of impressionable ladies in the audience, who later swelled his fan mail. Sunday said, "He (Rody) was a good judge of the kind of song that would be liked eventually, and we always respected his judgment." His hymns were more lighthearted than Ira Sankey's had been in Moody's time.

At every meeting Billy publicly fought a personal battle with the Devil, "the most formidable enemy the human race has to contend with." Billy's adversary was "the real, genuine, blazing-eyed, eleven-hoofed, forked-tail, old Devil. . . ." When he relegated such diverse characters as Charles Darwin, Madame de Pompadour and Henry VIII to the torments of hell, the spellbound audience could almost smell the brimstone.

At a revival in Philadelphia in 1915, John Wanamaker created a sensation when he charged into the audience dragging a drunken man for Billy to save.

During the same revival, a group of New York City ministers urged him to hold a campaign in Manhattan. He said that he would consent only if every Protestant church there lined up behind him. There were over eight hundred to unite, and the task was never successfully completed, but Billy compromised when John D. Rockefeller, Jr., offered his complete support.

Rockefeller provided the New York committee with the services of a nationally famous professional publicity organization. Sunday refused the committee's offer to rent Madison Square Garden for the revival, insisting upon his usual prefabricated tabernacle. When a suitable site could not be found, Mayor Mitchell agreed that a children's playground could be used, only to withdraw the offer because of the weight of adverse public opinion expressed in the press. At last Nell, now affectionately known to the nation as "Ma" Sunday, went to New York to settle the matter. She chose a vacant space upon which now stands the Presbyterian Hospital Medical Center at 168th Street and Broadway.

At that time the subway station had only one small elevator to transport passengers from 116 feet underground to street level. This problem was solved when the Fifth Avenue Bus Company under a new franchise was allowed a special routing for the benefit of revival crowds.

The New York Tabernacle was the most expensive ever built for Billy Sunday. Capable of holding 20,000 people, it cost $65,000. Four hundred workers took two months to build it.

On the opening night, April 1, 1917, Homer Rodeheaver, in fine form, first led the choir's singing of "Stand Up, Stand Up for Jesus," followed by "Brighten the Corner Where You Are," the tune of which the *New York Times* account described as "pre-syncopated jazz."

Finally, Billy appeared, "weighing about 145 pounds, and kept at the peak of athletic condition by a physical trainer who forms part of his retinue."

The *Times* report continues:

> He begins to dance like a shadow boxer. He slaps his hands together with a report like a broken electric lamp. He poses on one foot like a fast ball pitcher winding up. He jumps upon a chair. In the stress of his routine he may stand with one foot in the chair and another on the lectern. All the while he is flaying the "whisky kings," the German war lords, slackers, suffragettes or the local ministry. And, if his story of the sinner come home to salvation fits the gesture, he may emphasize the moral by throwing

himself on the floor with an outstretched arm groping for the home plate like a base-runner sliding safely in with a stolen run.

Then Billy told his favorite story of the country boy who went to a "fancy dress ball."

"I ought to call it a fancy undress ball," declared the evangelist, gesticulating wildly to the crowd below:

"There he was approached by a jezebel with hair like a raven's wing, a neck like a swan, teeth like a ledge of pearl in a snowdrift, wearing just enough clothing to pad a crutch, who, with difficulty, persuaded the young man to take his first glass of champagne.

"So the night wears on. Midnight, one o'clock, two A.M., and travelers see an agitated young man, wearing a linen duster over his clothes, walking up and down the station platform, taking a drink every once in a while from a pint flask and moaning, 'What will Mother say? My God, what will Mother say?'

"Four months later he died of delirium tremens and before he died he attacked his feeble and dear old mother and broke a chair over his father's head, and it took four strong men to hold him down on his deathbed."

New Yorkers could never forget some of Billy's vivid remarks. He once commented, "The women paint so much that if a man kisses one, he's liable to get painter's cholic."

During the aftermath of the New York revival, considered to be the peak of Billy's colorful career, the Federal Council of Churches reported only 200 permanent converts from the 68,000 claimed. To this charge Billy Sunday replied candidly, "I never yet have been satisfied with the results of any campaign I have ever conducted. No business house does as much business as it would like to!"

The total expenses of the New York campaign amounted

to $200,168.87. Actual collections at the meetings had
resulted in only $67,834.32. The remainder came from
what was classed as "contributions." These latter were
solicited by the committee from wealthy individuals and
businessmen.

The figures on the Billy Sunday revivals are almost
staggering. In 1916, before the revivals of that year in
Boston and Buffalo, and before the appearance in New
York, the *Baptist Watchman-Examiner* prepared the following table of results:

CITY	CONVERTS	THANK OFFERING
Philadelphia	41,724	$51,136
Baltimore	25,797	46,000
Pittsburgh	25,979	45,000
Trenton	16,810	32,358
Syracuse	21,155	23,255
Scranton	16,999	22,398
Wilkes-Barre	16,594	22,188
Columbus, Ohio	18,137	20,939
Omaha	13,022	19,000
Paterson	14,255	14,386
Wheeling	8,300	17,459
Toledo	7,686	15,423
Johnstown	11,829	14,000
McKeesport	10,023	13,438
Des Moines	10,200	13,000
East Liverpool	6,354	12,554
Canton, Ohio	5,640	12,500
Springfield	5,312	11,567
Erie	5,312	11,356
South Bend	6,398	11,200
Witchita	6,209	10,111
Denver	8,100	10,000
Kansas City	20,646	32,000

The roster of famous names responsible for promoting the Billy Sunday revivals reads like a page from *Who's Who*. Wealthy laymen liked to boast of the part they had personally played in bringing the evangelist to their cities.

In Philadelphia, Billy's famed campaign was made possible by that great friend of revivalism, John Wanamaker; John C. Winston, the publisher; Alba B. Johnson, president of the Baldwin Locomotive Works; and Cyrus H. K. Curtis. Allen C. Emery, of the Boston Wool Trade Association, is said to have brought Billy to that city. The millionaire silk manufacturer, George B. Arnold, took public credit for Billy's invitation to Paterson, New Jersey. At the same time another equally wealthy Paterson silk founder, Joseph Botsford Whitney, refused to entertain Sunday because of his platform criticism of Mary Baker Eddy, founder of Christian Science and a friend of his suffragette wife Martha Hasseltine. Suffragettes were also on Billy's black list.

Others among those whose names were associated with Sunday revivals were W. H. Donner, John M. Studebaker, S. S. Kresge, Joshua Levering, H. J. Heinz, Henry Leland, B. A. Walker, Henry Clay Frick, William Jennings Bryan, David Whitney, Anthony J. Drexel Biddle, George Wharton Pepper, H. P. Crowell, and even President Theodore Roosevelt, who invited Billy to his home.

President Woodrow Wilson received Billy Sunday at the White House, January 18, 1915, with the words "God bless you and your work." That day Billy had lunch with one of his idols, Secretary of State William Jennings Bryan. Later he addressed ministers and celebrities at Convention Hall on the theme "If Christ Came to Washington." He was introduced by Champ Clark, Speaker of the House of Representatives. Billy spoke without the aid of his usual acrobatics. Later, he was invited to hold a campaign in the city.

Bryan also maintained a mutual admiration for Billy, whose childlike faith in "the old-time religion" so completely matched his own.

The New York Campaign marked the end of Billy Sunday's phenomenal rise. After that, he continued to conduct revivals with considerable success, but the cities in which they were held continuously diminished in size. When he returned to New York after an almost complete absence of sixteen years, Billy said in his first sermon, "I have got just as much ginger and tabasco sauce for God as ever," but this time there was no specially built tabernacle. Billy divided his time equally between the Calvary Baptist Church and the Cornell Memorial Methodist Church.

With the coming of Prohibition, Billy Sunday's "Booze Sermon" gave away to another entitled "Crooks, Corkscrews, Bootleggers, and Whiskey Politicians—They Shall Not Pass."

Billy believed that Prohibition was a great blessing to the American nation and to the working man in particular. With the repeal of Prohibition he remarked somewhat sadly, "I can't continue to preach prohibition and preach the gospel. I'm not as young as I used to be and the load is too heavy. So I'm returning to my first love—preaching the gospel."

In his waning years Billy had much to say concerning the role of religion in the schools, a topic still much under discussion. "Education if divorced from religion leads to the spread of depravity," he said, "and is a greater menace to Christianity than Socialism—Communism—Bolshevism. Education is a false philosophy. We must not surrender our schools to atheism."

In 1935 he was given an honorary Doctor of Laws Degree at Bob Jones College, Greenville, South Carolina (it first began at Cleveland, Tennessee), where one of the female dormitories is named for Mrs. Sunday, *Nell Sunday Hall*. During her lifetime she was also elected to the Board of Trustees and given an honorary LL.D. degree. The Rodeheaver Auditorium is named for Homer Rodeheaver.

While preaching at Des Moines, Iowa in February 1933, Billy suffered a heart attack. When Harry Clarke ran to his assistance, the aging evangelist managed to say, "Don't let them go. They're lost. Give them the invitation. I'd rather die on my feet seeing them come than quit."

After a rest of some months, Billy was back again on his beloved Sawdust Trail, preaching his last sermon October 27, 1935, in a tiny church at Mishawaka, Indiana. He died suddenly, following another attack, while staying at the home of his brother-in-law, William J. Thompson, a Chicago florist.

Said "Ma" Sunday, "We had a doctor for him and he told me what to do. Tonight I brought Billy his dinner, and even got him some special ice cream. He seemed all right. But suddenly at 8 o'clock he said, 'Oh, I feel so dizzy.' Then he died. I'm glad it came like that because Billy always used to pray, 'O Lord, when I have to go, please make it quickly.' "

Chapter Six

EVANGELINE

General Evangeline Cory Booth

(1865-1950)

> "She [General Evangeline Booth] declares that it gives her a 'pang' to think that she must leave America for a time. But whenever she returns she may be assured of a welcome which her new honors may enhance but cannot make more cordial or sincere."
>
> *New York Times* editorial.

On Christmas morning, 1865, the six children of General William Booth and his wife, Catherine, were having breakfast at their home in Hammersmith, London. The church bells were ringing; snow lay thick on the ground. Suddenly their father, bearded and wearing the long frock coat then the mark of a nonconformist minister, walked in. He was carrying a wastepaper basket filled with straw. The children's faces reflected their excitement, for they thought he had brought them a puppy. Instead, lying in the basket, her tiny head generously supplied with dark hair, was a new baby sister.

Catherine Mumford Booth, often called "Mother of the Salvation Army," had been much affected by Harriet Beecher Stowe's "Uncle Tom's Cabin" and decided that the new arrival should be named "Little Eva" after one of its characters. William Booth, Founder of the Salvation Army, thought otherwise, for at the registrar's office he substituted "Evelyne" for "Little Eva." Years later, in the United States, Evelyne was persuaded by Frances Elizabeth Willard, founder of the Women's Christian Temperance Union, to call herself "Evangeline." That was the name by which she endeared herself to the world, and to Americans in particular. It seemed suited to the woman with the radiant face and sparkling personality.

As a child Evangeline was often reminded by her preaching mother that her middle name, "Cory," had strong associations with coal. John and Richard Cory, wealthy coal merchants from Cardiff, Wales, were active supporters of William Booth's Salvationist Movement, and had even allocated the profits from a ship affectionately named *The William Booth* to the cause. Unfortunately, it was wrecked off the coast of Bermuda, but even this did not deter the generous Corys from continuing their interest.

Life in the Booth household was a happy one, though disciplined to the customs of the times. William Booth was away, preaching in the field, for long intervals. Catherine believed in plenty of fresh air for her brood, which may account for the fact that all eight of the children survived the rigors of a Victorian upbringing. An eighth, Lucy, had been born after Evangeline.

Evangeline excelled at cricket, usually a boy's game, and

was especially good at batting. From her mother she inherited a deep love for animals. Her first pet was a dog
named "Nelson" after the famed Admiral of Trafalgar.
Unfortunately, when a nasty charwoman tried to smack
his young mistress one day, Nelson sprang to her protection
and bit the attacker. For some unexplained reason, the
faithful dog was led away to die. Evangeline was grief-
stricken. Hoping to appease her sorrow, William Booth
had Nelson's head and skin made into a rug, but poor
Evangeline only cried the more, so the pitiful object was
quickly removed.

Evangeline's next pet was a marmoset monkey named
"Jeannie," whose favorite pastime was to leap upon the
large, decorative hats of visiting ladies. Hoping to have
Jeannie mend her ways, Evangeline persuaded the kitchen
help to make the monkey a miniature Salvation Army uniform, complete with bonnet. But Catherine Booth was not
amused. Without speaking a word, she proceeded to undress
the monkey.

Evangeline demanded to know why.

"But, Eva, she doesn't live the life," explained her exas-
perated mother.

Mrs. Booth feared that because of the interest shown by
the public in her children they might be attracted to a
theatrical career instead of the religious life. Circuses she
felt to be especially dangerous, so the blinds of the Booth
home were tightly drawn when a circus was in the immediate vicinity. Once Evangeline lifted a blind just a little
to glimpse a splendid white horse. But William and Catherine were liberal where piano playing was concerned. They
noticed that various forms of music were described

throughout the Bible story, and their children grew up in an atmosphere of happy hymn-singing.

Evangeline loved preaching to her dolls, and was not even a teen-ager when she experienced "conversion." For years her parents had prayed for this time, which in the end came to Evangeline during the night hours. Early in the morning, she went to tell her parents. Kneeling between them, still wearing her nightgown, she gave special thanks to God.

Until 1861 William Booth had served as a minister in the Methodist New Connection. At that time he withdrew, and Catherine and he became independent evangelists, preaching in western England and Wales. It was to the terrible slums of London's East End that they were finally drawn to save "the unreached and unchurched."

Proclaiming that "the Lord Jesus Christ has by his suffering and death made an atonement for the whole world so that whatsoever will may be saved," Booth preached in tents, saloons, disused theaters, and even a Quaker cemetery.

First known as the Christian Movement and later developing into the Salvation Army, his organization ministered to everyone, regardless of race or religion. Members adopted military-type uniforms and Catherine designed Quaker-like bonnets for the women. The Army's meeting places were known as Citadels and Forts. Evangeline was brought up to believe that reading the Bible was in effect "taking one's rations." At fifteen she was made a sergeant in the Salvation Army. Growing into a very beautiful young woman, Evangeline received many proposals of marriage, but she always managed to say "No" diplomatically, and brush off the rumors of possible romances. A European, Prince Galitzin, proposed marriage when she was twenty-nine. He called her his "dear sweet Little Lamb."

As a full-fledged captain, Evangeline was no believer in a slap-dash type of preaching. In beautiful handwriting she copied out notes for her sermons. She believed that there should be a point to every address she gave, and that listeners should have some important message to take home with them. To fellow officers who tended to shout their addresses, she said gently, "Do not tread on velvet carpets with hobnailed boots."

One of her great admirers was John Bright, a Quaker statesman, who often attended her meetings. He was always fearful for Evangeline's health. "Take care of yourself, my child," he would tell her. "With that voice of yours, do not overtax your strength."

Other important statesmen became interested in Evangeline Booth, intrigued at the tales told of the way she could command attention at her meetings. She was invited to the Palace of Westminster to speak with Earl Cairns, Lord Shaftesbury, who had fought the battle for children employed down in the mines, and with Lord Onslow.

Lord Shaftesbury suggested that Evangeline, meekly seated in a red, leather-lined armchair, pretend him to be a drunkard. What would she say to him?

Replied Captain Evangeline, "I should tell you that you are a fine fellow, and I should want to know why you treated yourself like that—spoiling your looks and making yourself ridiculous. I should say to you that you are worth more than that and it is time you should know it."

When Catherine Booth, Evangeline's elder sister, descended upon Paris, the French called her "La Maréchale [the Field-Marshal's Lady]." Meanwhile, Evangeline started her own Salvationist life by selling *War Cry*, the army newspaper. Her stand was close to Liverpool Street Station, where she became a champion seller. At seventeen she was taking on assignments with Elijah Cadman, a converted chimney sweep. Cadman was always irate when a Salvationist was arrested for "disturbing the peace." To Evangeline's embarrassment, he would kneel on the front doorstep of the sentencing magistrate, praying aloud, "Lord, take him—take him away." Perhaps coincidentally, the Lord often obliged by the most drastic and final method.

The Salvation Army aimed to save the destitute, the alcoholics and the streetwalkers, but it worried Evangeline that she felt strangely removed from the very poor she wished to serve. Characteristically, she went to the crux of the matter by living the life of the downtrodden. At one time she became a flower girl, selling her violets from the steps in Piccadilly Circus, just as Eliza Doolittle in Shaw's *Pygmalion* would do. Another time she was a match-seller in the roughest section of Rotherhithe.

Religious street meetings were far from peaceful. Mobs employed by members of the liquor trade attempted to break up army meetings, and once Evangeline was dragged to the police court. Even the poor did not always want to be saved, especially by a "lady." They threw pails of hot water at her from their windows.

Evangeline served out a hard apprenticeship in the field, going wherever she was needed. At twenty-three, she was given command of the International Training College, Clapton, where cadets for the Salvation Army were trained. She defied convention by becoming the first woman Salvationist to ride a bicycle.

Whenever there was trouble in the ranks, General William Booth always said, "Send Eva," and Eva went. On one occasion she was dispatched to the town of Torquay in Devon, a seaside resort then much beloved by convalescents and invalids. Salvationists were being committed to prison for persisting in marching through the streets to the accompaniment of their militant-sounding bands.

Evangeline appeared twice at Torquay. On the first occasion she not only preached but when her aide-de-camp, a Captain Nicholls, sang, she accompanied him on the banjo. The second time 1500 people came to hear her address at the Royal Public Hall where Pounchee, a Ceylonese boy wearing a yellow turban, was among the "perfectly saved." Evangeline enthusiastically sang with her fellow members:

> The Dawlish Board speak well of us,
>   But Torquay runs us in,
> The L. B., says on Sabbath Day
>   To play it is a sin.
> And to bring about our fall,
>   With law do us assail,
> But like Silas and St. Paul
>   We sing and pray in jail.
> They grumble at the music,
>   They grumble at the drum,
> They grumble at our marching
>   To make the people come.
> They grumble at our uniform,
>   And say it's all display,
> But still we are the people
>   That are bound to win the day.

Twice during Evangeline's stay in Torquay she was presented with Court summonses. On one occasion, standing in the very dock recently occupied by a murderer, she said, "Gentlemen, you have seen some of these men. They have been brought before you in this court. You have imposed penalties on them for other offences than playing a trumpet or beating a drum. You have fined and imprisoned them for being drunk and disorderly, for thieving, for other wrongdoings. What is to be said of you as magistrates when these men who are known to you as offenders against the law come back changed, sober, orderly, honest, and guilty of nothing but praising God with instruments of music authorized by the Psalmist and blessed by the Saviour of mankind?"

Although Evangeline was convicted, the magistrates announced that she would receive no penalty.

Finally, Britain's House of Commons took up the matter of Torquay, the Salvation Army and General Evangeline. Once more she was asked to visit the Palace of Westminster, where again she made an impression with her dignified bearing, sincerity and youth. Calmly she answered all questions put to her by the select committee. Later, along with the whole Salvation Army, Evangeline had the pleasure of hearing that a clause relating to Sunday processions had been repealed by the passing of the Fowler Bill. In the Battle of Torquay she had been instrumental in winning a great victory. She became a Commander of the Salvation Army.

On Saturday afternoon, October 4, 1890, Catherine Mumford Booth, mother of the Salvation Army, died of cancer. On her death bed she told Evangeline, "My Christmas Box! Don't fret. You'll follow me! I'll watch for you."

Evangeline's second brother, Ballington Booth, and his wife, Maud, daughter of a Church of England clergyman, had been sent to the United States to take charge of the Salvation Army there. Ballington found no easy task awaiting him, for Americans were still suspicious of anything British, religious or otherwise. General William Booth operated from London where the Army's International Council was based. The Salvation Army in America and other countries still had to obey "rules and regulations" in an organization that itself had become international.

Toward the end of 1895 Ballington was ordered by his brother, Bramwell, then Acting Chief-of-Staff for their father, who was touring abroad, to relinquish his American command. Ballington countered by resigning from the Army on February 29, 1896. He immediately began to organize a rival body to be known as the Volunteers of America. William Booth, then in India, simply cabled Bramwell, "Send Eva."

Eva went, but she arrived in New York to find the front doors of the Salvation Army Headquarters on 14th Street barred against her. Ballington was inside, urging the Salvationists to join his Volunteers.

Acting on impulse, Evangeline ran around to the back of the building, climbed the fire escape and entered the building. Before her startled brother and the congregation, she appeared on the platform and insisted on being heard. With her usual eloquence, Evangeline persuaded the members to stay, and Ballington left the Salvation Army Headquarters for the last time.

But Ballington Booth's faction was not without support. When Evangeline mounted the platform for a meeting at Cooper Union she was booed and hissed. Stepping down, she returned a few minutes later draped in the Stars and Stripes. "Hiss that, if you dare," she challenged. Then, playing her concertina, she sang, "Over Jordan without fearing, He will leave me not alone."

Once more she won friends.

Evangeline's next important assignment was Canada. Her health was delicate and her father had been advised that she needed an open-air life with plenty of horseback riding. She landed in Toronto from the mission boat *William Booth*, June 11, 1896, bringing with her a horse and dogs, and rented a haunted house for a low rental because others were afraid to live in it.

She found the Canadian climate much to her liking, and her health improved so much that she was able to take part in the exciting Salvation Army operations in the Yukon, where gold had been discovered in 1896. She wrote her sister, the Maréchale, "The teeming multitudes mad for gold whom I saw on my recent tour, all heading for Alaska —they are indelibly branded in all their unsatisfied craving on my very soul."

Evangeline, as Field Commander, and the other officers, had to row nearly five hundred miles and travel afoot a considerable way, with bundles on their backs, to get to Dawson City. She visited Indians, conversing through interpreters with those who could not speak English. "When I listened to their hearty singing, 'His blood can make the vilest clean,' ringing through the woods where I conducted a midnight meeting in their little barracks, while the Captain held the boat, I found it difficult to see why we should hold back any longer from making them our own soldiers." The Indians had even made their own uniforms.

In Skagway, Evangeline and her officers were received hospitably and two log cabins were made available for their use. She marched her Salvationists to "Soapy Smith's Place," where she not only had the prospectors listening to her message of hope but had them on their knees singing "Home Sweet Home." "Soapy," who had once sold soap on the streets of Denver, Colorado, and was now the leader of a desperate gang of criminals, liked Evangeline. He told her over a cup of cocoa that as a boy his mother had taken him to Salvation Army meetings.

There were many converts in Alaska, but Soapy was not among them. He died from wounds sustained in a gun battle. However, Evangeline saw that fresh flowers were placed on his grave.

In 1903, Evangeline's sister, Emma, wife of Frederick Booth-Tucker (the men who married Booths assumed their wives' family names) was killed in a railway accident while on active duty with the Salvation Army. The New York *Daily News* called her funeral "the largest held in the city for a woman." On the way to Woodlawn Cemetery Evangeline collapsed with an attack of brain fever. Upon her recovery she succeeded to the American Command, for Emma's husband was too stricken by sorrow to be able to continue.

Evangeline Booth's thirty years of Command in the United States had begun. She became an American citizen. In her home, "Arcadia," named in honor of the legendary Evangeline, she could relax briefly and play her harmonium, which had belonged to Ira R. Sankey. When a well-wisher gave her a motorcar, she asked her father whether she should keep it. "Accept it," he replied, "and don't break your neck."

When Evangeline took over command of the Salvation Army in the United States in 1904, there were only 696 stations. In 1934, she could proudly count more than 4,500.

In New York she was horrified to find 70,000 children going to school without breakfast . . . This she set out to remedy. In 1933, 650,000 had food baskets to take home on Christmas Day. When the John D. Rockefeller, Jr., agency investigated the Salvation Army in America as an organization that depended upon public monies to exist, they declared it "fundamentally spiritual in its aim."

Evangeline, on the advice of John Wanamaker, reserved her own speaking appearances for special occasions. He said that people should always be made to consider it a privilege to hear her. In this way, with advancing years, she was able to conserve her strength for occasions where her presence would do the most good. Presidents received her, and William Howard Taft once came to hear her preach. She filled the Hollywood Bowl to its capacity. In 1912 she gave the invocation at the Democratic Convention in Chicago when Theodore Roosevelt received the nomination. Emperor Hirohito saluted her in the royal gardens at Tokyo.

During the First World War, Evangeline Booth was particularly active. Before the United States entered the conflict in 1917, Salvationists conducted an old linen campaign, collecting, rolling and sterilizing bandages for shipment to the battlefields of France.

After America joined the fray, Evangeline decided upon quality instead of quantity. The girls she sent to the front were fully trained, right down to their Red Cross diplomas. They saved souls, baked pies and doughnuts, tended the dying and even helped the soldiers save their money. When General Pershing asked for a homemade apple pie, his French chef could not oblige, but one of Evangeline's lassies saved the day.

Long after hostilities had ceased—in 1927—Evangeline Booth visited France, where the work of her girls was well remembered. She prayed at the Arc de Triomphe; and at a great thanksgiving service, on the tenth anniversary of

America's entering the war, she was escorted up the aisle with General John J. Pershing and Marshall Ferdinand Foch on either side.

In 1920, General Bramwell Booth, who had succeeded their father as Commander-in-Chief of the Salvation Army upon his death in 1912, recalled his sister Evangeline from America for good. He told her, "You cannot expect to remain at the head of the organization [in the U.S.A.,] all the rest of your life." But Evangeline persuaded him to allow her to stay two more years.

Then, in 1922, when she was recuperating from a serious throat operation, she was shocked to be informed through the *New York World*, a newspaper, that she had been removed as Commander in the United States. There was no mention of further service. Visibly upset, Evangeline Booth announced to reporters, "I shall obey the order when the date is set for me to go."

Protests to Bramwell poured in from all parts of the world. He felt obliged to issue a statement, maintaining, "I have had no thought of an immediate farewell." Evangeline's prestige in the eyes of the world, and America in particular, was enhanced more than ever. Her submission to orders, unjust as they were, was admired by thousands of wellwishers who were not Salvationsts.

In 1929, General Bramwell Booth himself was deposed by the High Council of the Salvation Army, and Edward J. Higgins was elected to succeed him. Evangeline returned to her beloved America, but not for long. General Higgins retired in 1934, and Evangeline was chosen Commander-in-Chief in his place. The fourth general of the Salvation Army, returning from the High Council in London that had elected her, was given a tremendous welcome in New

York. Ruth Nichols scattered roses from her plane and tugs roared as Evangeline's ship entered the harbor. Mayor Fiorello La Guardia led the reception committee. Together they drove up Broadway while ticker tape fell like rain from office windows above.

William Booth had once written Evangeline, "Your career has been a remarkable one, but destiny, unless I am mistaken, has something in store for you more wonderful still."

At that moment, Evangeline knew he was right.

Chapter Seven

PROPHET IN A
LONG FUR COAT

"Daddy" Grace

(1883=1960)

"They say he has some three million ecstatic followers,
that he bottles and sells the water he bathes in, that
he once performed mass baptisms with a fire hose and
that his income is in the millions—and untaxed."

THE AUGUSTA HERALD

"Sweet Daddy" Grace, or Charles Manuel Grace, was born
in Portugal's Cape Verde Islands in 1883. He came to the
United States in 1903 to settle at New Bedford, Massachusetts. At one time he was a cranberry picker.

At the time of his death he was reported to have had
twenty-five million dollars. As Bishop (self-appointed) and
Founder of the Church of the Rock of Apostolic Faith, he
operated three hundred institutions in America for worship-

pers. With few exceptions, his followers were colored people. His church, known as "The House of Prayer for All
People," was painted red, white and blue, as were the five-
inch fingernails on his left hand. One of the most spectacular
of all modern evangelists, "Sweet Daddy" had three million
followers in more than sixty cities. Elegantly dressed during
the cold weather in an ankle-length mink coat, he often
declared, "I am all people's man. I am the boy friend of the
world!"

Daddy Grace had not remained an immigrant cranberry
picker for long. In 1926 he started his church at Charlotte,
North Carolina, baptizing his followers in a local pond,
and the faithful loved him, showering dollar bills in his
pathway. They were still doing it many years later when
the Augusta House of Prayer for All People was celebrating its thirtieth anniversary.

In 1926, "Sweet Daddy" had conducted services in a
tent, later graduating to a barnlike building with a dirt
floor; When he returned in 1956, rich, powerful and a
celebrity, his House of Prayer occupied a handsome two-
story edifice reported to have cost $250,000.

The parade through Augusta upon that occasion included
three bands, and the participants were variously attired in
immaculate business suits, elaborate military-style uniforms
or flowing white robes. Daddy Grace himself was the star
attraction, sitting comfortably in an armchair on a care-
fully-shaded float. Smiling graciously as the people strewed
rose petals and dollar bills before him, "Sweet Daddy"
helped himself to peanuts from a paper sack, and occasionally threw one to the crowd.

Behind him, his Royal Guard stood rigidly at attention
wearing a powder blue uniform trimmed with red braid.

On Daddy Grace's own right shoulder was a gold aglet. As the cavalcade reached the House of Prayer for All People, an announcer told the four thousand colored people waiting eagerly for a glimpse of their spiritual leader, "Behold! He is here. Look upon him!"

As "Sweet Daddy" was carried to the front of the church, where another armchair throne awaited him, a brass band aided by cymbals and tambourines struck up a pulse-quickening, spine-tingling musical arrangement in 6/8 time which *The Augusta Herald* described as being "like syncopated ruffles and drums for a visiting 25-star General."

While "Sweet Daddy" ascended his throne, a church elder cried, "We call him Daddy!"

A chorus of happy, expectant voices replied with one accord: "We call him Daddy!"

Then, according to *The Augusta Herald*, "The Congregation rose as a man and a long, tortuous snake-dance began up and down the aisles."

"Sweet Daddy" sat watching the gyrations of the faithful, his solid gold belt and out-size emerald ring flashing in the light.

Says newspaperman Anthony Harrigan, "When the Bishop rose to speak, the reaction was markedly similar to Elvis Presley's effect on an audience of teen-agers. High-pitched screams rent the air; the whole congregation emitted a great common sigh."

Said "Sweet Daddy," "This room is happy."

Replied the people, "Amen! Amen!"

Then "Sweet Daddy" spoke again. "These walls are happy," and again the same answer came:

"Amen! Amen!"

"This ceiling is happy."

"Amen! Amen!"

Finally said "Sweet Daddy," with resignation, "And the band is happy!"

After each loud "Amen," the band responded with a crescendo of wild chords. Of the magnetic Bishop, Harrigan declared, " 'Daddy Grace' has to be seen to be appreciated. He knows it."

"Sweet Daddy" did know it. By the time he was sixty years old, he had taught himself to speak six languages, including Hebrew. He was described by the press as "an expert linguist."

Although he had an administrative headquarters for his church in Washington, he seldom had time to visit it. "I have no home," he once said. "I travel each of the forty-eight states and Cuba. I bring the word of God, unchanged, to the House of Prayer for All People"—regardless of creed, race or color. Did you see the crowds today? Weren't they pretty? Weren't they wonderful?"

Daddy Grace traveled in a bright blue Cadillac as part of an eleven-car convoy, always accompained by a staff of elders of his church. Six weeks every year he spent in Cuba, where his confidential secretary once told the press, "There was some talk of making him president."

Elder Jay Rayner, of his congregation, commented, " 'Daddy' Grace succeeds in giving many Negroes what they want in religious leadership, though the more orthodox preachers bitterly condemn him."

"Sweet Daddy's" story of success in evangelism seems to lie more in his outgoing personality, flare for the spectacular and canny business sense than in his actual preaching ability. In thirty years he acquired a large amount of valuable property in the major American cities, and abroad including a $450,000 eighty-five room mansion in Los Angeles, where he was reportedly fanned with palm leaves. He purchased the Eldorado Towers, New York City, then said to be the tallest apartment building in the world. His House of Prayer in Charlotte could boast such extra amenities as a flourishing cafeteria and a beauty parlor that sold "Sweet Daddy Grace" cold cream. Hair lotions, soap and toothpaste bearing his name enjoyed large sales. In his cafeteria he used eggs from his Cuban hatchery and coffee from his own Brazilian plantation.

Daddy Grace's fame and reputed wealth often made him the target for lawsuits. The most widely publicized one ended on January 14, 1958, when "Sweet Daddy" won the case against a fifty-seven year old retired Georgia schoolteacher, Mrs. Louvenia Royster, who said he was her husband. Claiming him to be John Royster, the father of her daughter, she demanded alimony and support. Mrs. Royster asserted that she had been deserted by "Sweet Daddy" in 1928.

The case was tried in Washington, D. C., where Judge Alexander Holtzoff announced, "You can call him Grace or Royster but don't call him Daddy. Please don't call people by their nicknames in this court."

"Sweet Daddy" stole the show by ascending the witness stand resplendent in a purple cutaway with gold-trimmed cuffs and epaulets to match, and an elegant blue and yellow cravat with a superimposed golden cross.

Judge Holtzoff felt obliged to tell "Sweet Daddy" that he must stop accepting contributions in the Federal courtroom. However there was nothing he could do to prevent the Bishop from handing out candy bars to anybody he thought looked hungry. "Sweet Daddy's" blue and gold uniformed guards attended him in court.

On the very day that Mrs. Royster claimed to have become "Sweet Daddy's" bride, his attorney, Franklyn Yasmer, declared, the supposed bridegroom was on the way to Jerusalem. He even had a passport to prove it. Yasmer suggested that the suit had been brought because of the Bishop's "widespread publicity."

Retorted the judge, "I guess I have been ignorant. I never heard about the defendant until yesterday."

During the trial a letter was received from another woman, Mrs. Jennie Grace of New Bedford, Massachusetts, saying that she was the bishop's first wife and that he "left me many years ago" after the birth of two children.

"I never signed no divorce paper," she complained. "I may tell more about it later."

"Never heard of her," snapped "Sweet Daddy," and continued to polish his fingernails.

To the assertions of this new "wife" Yasmer replied by calling his client "a target, a sitting duck, for all kinds of claims. He gets a lot of letters like this from women who call him 'my spiritual husband, my heavenly husband'! Women move into his home, and he has to throw them out."

After handing down a lengthy decision, the judge dismissed Mrs. Royster's claim. "Sweet Daddy" seemed unaware of the verdict until reporters told him he had won the case. Then, raising his flamboyantly decorated left hand, he proclaimed, "There's a God up there! I ought to shake the judge's hand."

Just as persuasive in the courtroom as in the pulpit,

"Sweet Daddy" had the satisfaction of seeing another case against him thrown out, after he had been indicted for allegedly paying $41 tax upon an income of $190,000.

"Sweet Daddy's" death in a Los Angeles hospital, January 12, 1960, as a result of a heart attack and stroke, was the occasion of much sorrow among his many thousands of widely scattered followers, who, according to an editorial in the Charleston, S.C., *News and Courier*, "revered him as a modern Moses." Following funeral services in Charlotte, his body was taken back to New Bedford "for entombment."

In February, 1960, Uncle Sam froze Daddy Grace's large estate with many court liens, claiming nearly six million dollars in unpaid income tax from the late-lamented preacher.

The Internal Revenue Service said that the Bishop had controlled ninety bank and savings-and-loan accounts with balances totaling over $1.8 million. He had never become a United States citizen. They further claimed that he had placed his real estate holdings in the name of "The Church of the House of Prayer for All People, Bishop Charles M. Grace, trustee."

Said the Associated Press:

> The bill for $5,966,000 in taxes for the years 1945 through 1956 is one of the largest ever entered by the Internal Revenue Service against an individual. The sums claimed range from $108,914 for 1945 to $1,531,063 for 1960.

Eventually, in June, 1961, peace was declared between "Sweet Daddy's" estate and the Internal Revenue Service, which accepted $1.94 million in full settlement, explaining that "Considerable confusion exists over his personal income and that belonging to his 350 churches in 60 cities which was non-taxable."

"Sweet Daddy" had the last laugh on his critics. He had willed back to his church most of those green dollar bills he had so often been accused of hoarding.

Chapter Eight

SISTER

Aimee Semple McPherson

(1890-1944)

"She could have bought oil wells—
She might have built palatial homes—
But she built a temple of service—
Where whosoever might come . . .
The needy—the sick—the discouraged—
And find help and solace in their hour of need . . ."

So reads her epitaph in the memorial brochure, "A Medal for Sister." Known to the world as Aimee Semple McPherson, back in the Roaring Twenties she made headlines comparable to those of Billy Graham.

"From Milkpail to Pulpit," the title of one her recordings, sums up the story of her life. Aimee was born on October 9, 1890, in a typical gabled Canadian farmhouse five miles from Ingersoll, Ontario. Her father, James Morgan Kennedy, was a descendant of Methodist ministers; her dynamic mother, Minnie Peaue Kennedy, had grown

up in the home of a Salvation Army Captain and his wife.
Aimee Elizabeth was their only child.

Mrs. Kennedy had served both at home and overseas
with the Salvation Army. When Aimee was born she dedicated her daughter to God's service, using the words once
spoken by Hannah, mother of Samuel: *"For this child I
prayed; and the Lord hath given me my petition, which I
asked of him: Therefore also I have lent [her] to the Lord;
as long as [she] liveth [she] shall be lent to the Lord."*

Aimee's religious training started early. At three weeks
she accompanied her mother to a local Salvation Army
jubilee; at six weeks she was carried onto the platform!

Life on the farm was a happy one. Aimee grew up loving
the countryside and enjoying the companionship of birds
and animals. Like other farmers' daughters, she was brought
up to do her full share of the chores. She writes, in *The
Story of My Life*, of "searching for eggs in the nests of
hens that insisted upon playing hide and seek . . . the
peep of chilled baby turkeys in gathered apron, borne into
the farmhouse to the reviving warmth before an open oven
door, securely wrapped in a woolen shawl . . . lighting
the lamps and spreading the red tablecloth for the evening
meal."

Aimee rode to public school on Flossie, the mare, and
her pets were a pet pigeon named Jenny, a dignified cat
called Whitetail, and an owl that "blinked and blinked"
from his perch on the back of a kitchen chair. Aimee's
childhood ambition was not unusual; she wanted to be an
actress. There was a "pleasant huskiness" in the quality of
her voice.

As a seventeen-year-old she was troubled in her mind
concerning the subject of evolution, then a leading topic.
Doubting the truth of her religious beliefs, Aimee read all

that was available on the subject, including Darwin, Voltaire and Paine. At last, in desperation, she took the bull by the horns and wrote the *Family Herald and Weekly Star* in Montreal. Her published letter brought replies from hundreds of readers, including an archbishop. It seemed fate that she should attend Robert James Semple's revival meeting at the time she was still disturbed over the Bible's veracity. Going to scoff, instead she sat spellbound by the speaker. "Repent and be baptized, every one of you, in the name of Jesus Christ, for the remission of sins, and ye shall receive the gift of the Holy Ghost."

To Aimee, it seemed that this message was directed especially at her. For three days she debated the sermon in her mind. Then, while driving home through the snow in the family cutter, she surrendered her life to Christ and was "wonderfully saved."

Even after the Reverend Robert Semple had completed his revival campaign in Ingersoll, Aimee still kept in touch by correspondence. Later, when she arrived at the home of a mutual friend to care for two children who were stricken by typhoid fever, she found the evangelist already there. He had journeyed from Stratford, Ontario.

Telling her of his plans to be a missionary in the Far East, Robert Semple proceeded to show her a map of the Orient. Then, without any prior warning, he asked Aimee to marry him. With her heart "pounding like a trip-hammer" she just as spontaneously accepted his offer.

Robert was six feet tall and blue-eyed, with a mass of fair hair. Standing there, Bible in hand, he filled Aimee Kennedy's ideal of a man.

Aimee's parents approved the match wholeheartedly. Ever since she had dedicated her daughter to the Lord, Minnie believed Aimee destined for great things, and her child's marriage to a missionary was a union after her own heart. She immediately began planning for a wedding Aimee would always remember.

With the typical friendliness of Canadian farm folk, the neighboring women came in to help. While Aimee was fitted for her trousseau, willing hands helped Minnie prepare the wedding feast. Childhood friends fashioned a wedding bower of roses, hydrangeas and goldenglow, and after the ceremony on August 12, 1908, the Reverend and Mrs. Robert Semple drove to the railroad station in a ribbon-bedecked, horse-drawn carriage. Aimee never forgot that beautiful drive. The corn was almost ripe; the apple trees were laden with fruit.

But Robert's work did not allow time for a honeymoon. The newlyweds set out on a revival tour, with Chicago on their itinerary. Afterward, they set sail on the *Empress of Ireland* from St. John, New Brunswick, bound for Ireland by way of Liverpool. Robert had the dual purpose of introducing to his Scottish-Irish parents their new daughter-in-law and conducting revival meetings in Belfast.

Later, when Robert preached in London, his bride played the piano. As they left England, bound for the Orient, well-wishers ashore sang, "God be with you till we meet again."

It was a long, pleasant journey. Robert spent hours reading aloud from his favorite *Pilgrim's Progress*, and as the ship passed through the Red Sea the young Semples stood on deck wondering where Pharoah had actually crossed in pursuit of the Israelites. In Ceylon the lepers depressed Aimee as they begged for alms with mutilated hands. India she thought "superstition-ridden, beautiful and ugly, lovely and horrible!" A simoon overtook their ship in the Indian Ocean, and for two days they rode out the storm.

Upon reaching Hong Kong Robert gave silent thanks from the ship's prow for their safe deliverance. He was anxious to reach the Chinese mainland where souls were waiting to be saved.

In Hong Kong, the young Semples were warmly greeted by other missionaries already established there, who took them to see the native markets, where the fly-infested meat stands and squirrels that resembled rats horrified Aimee. However, if she was homesick she never showed it.

The Semples' first home, in Hong Kong, was built next to a Hindu temple. Its furnishings were of necessity simple, but the Semples hired a Chinese cook for the equivalent of ten cents a day and set about, with the exuberance of youth, studying the native language for several hours every day. They were undaunted when told that sometimes it took twenty years to master a single dialect, and that there were several hundred different ones.

Life next to a temple had its special problems, for cremations were held under their kitchen window. Aimee found the hot weather particularly oppressive, also, since she was expecting her first child. She hung dampened sheets at the windows, hoping that they might cool the air. Malaria was rampant in the area, and when both husband and wife sickened at the same time they found it necessary to return to Hong Kong from a mission near Macao, where they had been working, for hospitalization.

Robert was so ill when they arrived that he had to be carried on a litter to the English sanatorium. There he and Aimee were placed in separate wards, from which they exchanged notes to mark their second wedding anniversary.

Aimee's attack of malaria was mild compared with her husband's, and she was allowed up and could visit him for short periods; but at the end of a week Robert had weakened considerably. Just three months after their arrival in the Orient, he died.

A month later Roberta Star Semple was born.

With her six-weeks-old daughter, Aimee returned to America on the *Empress of China*. Evangelist friends in Chicago had paid for Robert's funeral and Aimee's parents had cabled the passage money home. Aimee's fellow passengers were kind to her and gave her clothing for baby Roberta. When the ship berthed at San Francisco, Aimee was presented with sixty-seven dollars collected by the other travelers, which proved just enough to get her to her parents' home in New York.

Desperately lonely, Aimee found solace in mission work, and visited the mission in Chicago where Robert had preached. But constant traveling was not good for the young baby, and a doctor advised Aimee to make a quiet home for the child. A few years later she married Harold Stewart McPherson, of Providence, Rhode Island, and Rolf Kennedy McPherson was born of this union.

Even then, Aimee's restless spirit found little consolation. Ill-health dogged her, and she underwent two major operations. It seemed to her that God was chastising her for having deserted the field of evangelism, and she was plagued by the verse from the Bible, *But Jonah rose up to flee unto Tarshish from the presence of the Lord.*

During Aimee's adolescence her mother had often reminded her that as a baby she had been dedicated to God. Now, at death's door in the hospital, she rededicated herself to His service.

Visiting her parents' Ingersoll farmhouse, Aimee, now known as Sister McPherson, explained her desire to return to religious work. Her delighted mother agreed to take charge of the children, and Aimee set out for Kitchener, where a big tent revival meeting was being held.

After the first meeting she offered her services to the campaign leaders, who assigned her to wash the dishes. Later she graduated to playing the piano where, according to her own account, she "hit every key from top to bottom." So useful did Sister McPherson become that she was asked by the evangelist's wife to help in the London (Ontario) campaign. She even painted a banner: COME TO THE GREAT CAMP MEETING.

In August, 1915, Aimee was invited to conduct Revival Services at a Pentecostal mission, where her husband assisted her, and here her world-wide ministry began.

Disappointed with her first small congregation inside the tiny church, Sister McPherson, chair in hand, marched to the main corner of town, where the sight of a beautiful woman preaching from a street corner naturally drew a crowd of men and women. Then, like the Pied Piper of old, Aimee led them into the church.

Not until the end of the first week did she have the courage to take up her first collection, which amounted to sixty-five dollars. By this time, her revival meetings had grown to such proportions that they had to be held on a large lawn. With the collection money, Aimee purchased a second-hand tent, but it proved to be badly mildewed and full of holes.

Undaunted, Sister McPherson, assisted by some of the faithful, worked hours to patch it. Finally the tent was raised into position, gaily camouflaged with hand-painted texts. In the middle of her first sermon a high wind caused it to sag dangerously. The congregation had no time to panic, for the lady evangelist screamed, "In the name of the Lord, I command you to stay there 'til the meeting is over!"

"Believe it or not," Aimee recalls, "that tent caught on a protruding nail and stayed!"

From Mount Forest, Aimee and Harold, with a brand new tent, returned to Providence, where she conducted her second revival, afterward, "working" the entire Eastern Seaboard. During the summer she went as far north as Maine, following the birds to Florida in the winter, where she stayed for two years. Roberta and Rolf now traveled, too, sleeping in tents and sharing their mother's ministry. With her "Gospel Auto," Sister was already becoming a popular figure in the home mission field. Those who disapproved of women preachers were often the first to be "saved" when they attended her services.

Aimee was sustained by free will offerings. If she was short of funds the Lord always seemed to provide. She prayed for a typewriter to write her articles for religious magazines, and a machine arrived from an unexpected source. When she was without funds for food in Jacksonville a large box of used clothing arrived from Corona, Long Island, where she had recently been preaching, and she found the sleeves and pockets of a jacket on top crammed with crackers and sardines. She thought of the "loaves and fishes" while eating supper that night.

In June 1917, Sister published her own magazine, *Bridal Call*, writing the entire contents herself. One of her most famous sermons was entitled, "The Bride in Her Veil of Types and Shadows," based on the text, "Come hither, I will shew thee the bride, the Lamb's wife" (*Revelations* 21:9). These words seemed to suggest an appropriate banner-head for her new publication. Only two years before, her health had so deteriorated that she had been at death's door. Now her energy seemed limitless.

When McPherson ceased working with Aimee in 1918 she continued alone. The sawdust trail was no bed of roses. Once, in the swamps of Georgia, Sister Aimee was almost eaten alive by mosquitoes. On another occasion her battered gospel-auto firmly stuck in the mud so that even her petticoats enchained around the wheels failed to make them budge, and she had to trudge through the heavy rain in search of help, leaving the children asleep in the car. The fact that she had no dependable financial support never worried Aimee McPherson. She had a job with the Lord, and nothing was going to stop her!

In 1918 she was joined by her mother, whose shrewd business sense and executive ability combined with Aimee's platform appeal, dynamic drive and beauty made them a powerful team.

Los Angeles was their Mecca, but to get there the two women had to drive all the way across the continent. At night, they camped with the two children by the roadside.

People were very kind. Many of them had become acquainted with the lady evangelist through *Bridal Call*. Across prairie, desert and mountain passes the women slowly progressed, until at last the orange groves of California lay stretched out like the Promised Land to greet them.

Los Angeles proved fruitful for Aimee's ministry. She preached downtown at Victoria Hall which, according to her own count, seated about a thousand people, and often the overflow could not be accommodated.

Aimee decided to make Los Angeles her headquarters, but between 1918 and 1923 she crossed the United States with her mother eight times, conducting services in tents, churches, theaters and auditoriums. Revivals were held in Philadelphia, San Francisco, Baltimore, San Diego, Washington, D.C., Dayton, Denver, Montreal, Hartford, the Bronx, Indianapolis and St. Louis. At San Francisco in April, 1922, she broadcast the first sermon given on the air, blazing the way as a pioneer radio preacher.

In 1920 she was the chief attraction at a Bronx revival meeting, where her headquarters was a large "tabernacle tent" erected in a field. On the first night she attracted a tough element of "giggling, gum-chewing girls and cigar-smoking boys," but the next evening her audience was more appreciative. Each afternoon the children were invited, many of them coming in ragged and poor from the streets. On Saturdays Aimee served them ice cream and chocolate cake. A notable feature of her lifelong ministry was her generosity to the underprivileged.

In spite of teeming rain that lasted eight days, Sister Aimee, like Noah of old, withstood the deluge in her own canvas ark. Congregations were obliged to use umbrellas as they sang, for even the tent leaked. Well-wishers built Sister a plank bridge to the platform to protect her feet from the mud.

In Baltimore, a mentally disturbed woman almost broke up a meeting. Screaming "Praise the Lord," she marched up the aisle, knocking off the lady worshippers' outsize hats. Aimee had the presence of mind to tell a choir member quickly to intercept the intruder and lead her out before the revival was ruined. It turned out that the unfortunate creature believed herself to be a preacher.

At San Diego, California, in 1921, Aimee was invited to preach during intermission, from a boxing arena. "Oh, Lord help us," she thought, standing under the glare of arc lights. She quelled the jeers and catcalls of the noisy fight fans by her sincerity, and took the opportunity of inviting everyone to attend her revival the next evening in the same arena.

Many persons testified to the newspapers that they had actually been healed of physical afflictions during Sister Aimee's services. At San Diego, a veteran of the Civil War insisted that he could hear again, although years before his ear drums had been punctured by the burst of a shell.

One of Sister's most successful revivals began at the People's Tabernacle, Denver, Colorado, and continued at the 15,000-capacity municipal auditorium when the congregations became too large. Determined to get seats the next day, worshippers barricaded themselves overnight in the rest rooms. The altar calls received such enthusiastic response that Sister had two instead of the customary one. Often when she called for "sinners and backsliders" half the congregation accepted her invitation to come forward.

The healing sessions at the Denver revival were memorable. Even hard-boiled reporters were noticeably touched. On June 23, 1921, *The Denver Post* headlined its lead story CHILD WITH NECK TUMOR CURED BY HEALING HAND OF EVANGELIST, and continued with an account of a number of cures claimed by attenders. Two months later, ten cases chosen at random were interviewed by reporters. Of these, six declared that their cures had been permanent and that their conditions had steadily improved since that time; one, that he had suffered no setback; two, that they had experienced what they considered temporary relapses; only one that his condition was worse and that the seeming cure was due to excitement and elation.

A close observer of Sister Aimee commented after this campaign,

Frankly, I doubt that that meeting should be chosen as exactly typical of her [Sister's] evangelistic preaching, except as to the thronging crowds, the many converts, etc. These are my reasons: The Gospel in its fullness has many facets, of which prayer for the sick is but one. Whenever in this day and age some long neglected facet is revived and preached again, the revival of it is always attended by most astonishing evidences that do not, however, continue in their intensity, but taper off to an even plane. Much as the winds and the tongues of fire attested the first advent of the Holy Spirit in the Upper Room.

It was at Oakland, California, during her summer campaign of 1922 that Aimee Semple McPherson proclaimed to the world her "Foursquare Gospel" (in 1927 her movement was incorporated under the title of "International Church of the Foursquare Gospel"). A description from the Book of Ezekiel guided her in making such a choice of name: *As for the likeness of their faces, they four had the face of a man, and the face of a lion, on the right side: and they four had the face of an ox on the left side; they four also had the face of an eagle.*

This vision seemed to Sister Aimee to typify the fourfold ministry of Jesus embracing His roles as Saviour of the World; Baptizer with the Holy Ghost; Great Physician and Healer of our bodies; and Coming King of Kings.

She compiled a *Declaration of Faith* comprising twenty-two special points, including pronouncements on

The Holy Scriptures: ". . . that the Holy Bible is the Word of the living God; true, immutable, steadfast, unchangeable, as its author, the Lord Jehovah."

The Eternal Godhead: ". . . that there is but one true and living God . . ."

Salvation Through Grace: ". . . that the salvation of sinners is wholly through grace; that we have no righteousness or goodness of our own wherewith to seek divine favor . . ."

The New Birth: ". . . that the change which takes place in the heart and life at conversion is a very real one; that the sinner is then born again in such a glorious and transforming manner that old things are passed away and all things are become new . . ."

Baptism and the Lord's Supper: ". . . that water baptism in the name of the Father and of the Son and of the Holy Ghost, according to the command of our Lord, is a blessed outward sign of an inward work; . . . . . We believe in the commemoration and observing of the Lord's supper . . ."

Moderation: ". . . that the moderation of the believer should be known of all men; that his experience and daily walk should never lead him into extremes, fanaticisms, unseemly manisfestations, back-bitings, murmerings . . ."

Divine Healing: ". . . that divine healing is the power of the Lord Jesus Christ to heal the sick and the afflicted in answer to believing prayer . . ."

The Second Coming of Christ: ". . . that the second coming of Christ is personal and imminent . . ."

Under the heading of *Evangelism* Sister McPherson asserts:

We believe that . . . the redeemed children of the Lord Jehovah should rise and shine forth as a light that cannot be hid, a city set upon a hill, speeding forth the gospel to the ends of the earth, girding the globe with the message of salvation, declaring with burning zeal and earnestness the whole council of God . . . that soul winning is the one big business of the church upon earth . . .

Unlike most famous evangelists, Aimee Semple McPherson had decided to form a completely new sect. Now all she needed was a permanent home for her church. She prayed for the day that her Foursquare Gospel would be thus established.

She herself discovered the site for Angelus Temple—"the most beautiful spot for the house of the Lord that I have ever seen"—near Echo Park, Los Angeles. In April, 1921, with only $5,000 in cash, construction began. The new temple would be a Class A fireproof building containing seats for over five thousand people. Wielding an outsize shovel, a radiantly happy Sister broke ground for the project, watched by her approving mother and her daughter, Roberta, now a pretty young girl with corkscrew curls.

While work was still in progress, Aimee sailed for Australia to conduct a campaign. Although she was distressed upon arrival to find that she had been invited by an ostracized sect unpopular with other Christian groups, she was hard at work only twenty-four hours after disembarking from her four-week journey. What might have been a fiasco became instead a successful campaign.

Getting back to what she defined as "the fundamental truths concerning the inspiration of the Scriptures," she drew large congregations and was encouraged by the ministers and laymen of various denominations who volunteered their help. She preached in Melbourne, Adelaide and Sydney before returning to America. En route home, she designed the eight stained glass windows, each thirty feet high, for Angelus Temple. No two were alike. By modern standards these windows are of high quality, depicting such scenes as the Christ Child in the stable at Bethlehem, the baptism of Jesus by John the Baptist in the River Jordan, and Jesus in a seamless dress comforting a woman taken in sin. Aimee's inspiration came from the Song of Solomon, 2:9: *He looketh forth at the windows.*

Arriving in Los Angeles, she found the shell of the handsome building of concrete and steel far advanced. Friends all over the United States and Canada had sent gifts to help build Sister's Temple for the Lord.

The two-balconied edifice was crowned with what was said to be the largest unsupported dome in North America. The main entrance doors were of crystal. On dedication day, January 1, 1923, the great organ played "Open the Gates of the Temple!"

Sister's voice had faltered when, visibly moved, she spread mortar upon the dedication stones. Then, lifted onto a temporary platform, she read aloud the story of the dedication of Solomon's temple in Jerusalem.

Angelus Temple prospered from the very beginning. Each week Sister personally conducted twenty-one services. On February 6, 1924, she broadcast the first message over her own radio station, KFSG, the initials standing for "Kall Four Square Gospel."

Vast crowds attended the religious plays, tableaux and operas that she presented on the temple's full-size stage, employing with great success the lighting effects of a New York theater. In reality, she had taken religion back to the days of the medieval morality and miracle plays.

Sister was advertised on a marquee similar to those on Broadway, with her white-robed, more-than-life-size figure placed above. Hollywood movie moguls knew better than to arrange a premiere to coincide with one of her Biblical extravaganzas.

A Prayer Tower became a feature of the Temple. Here the women members took prayer watches by day and men at night. For the first anniversary of Angelus Temple, Sister baked a birthday cake made from Bible ingredients—

flour as mentioned I Kings 4:22; sugar from Jeremiah 6:20; butter from Judges 5:25, etc. With the exception of home-grown raisins, the rest of the fruit was imported from Italy. Baked as a replica of the Temple, it weighed over three hundred pounds. One hundred pounds of powdered sugar alone had been used for the icing. In ten minutes sixty ushers had passed pieces of cake to 5,500 people.

A Bible College begun in March, 1923, in Angelus Temple's "120 Room" was of necessity in September, 1924, expanded to the "500 Room." The five-story School and Administration Building near the Temple were opened in January, 1926. Then Sister started a weekly magazine, *Crusader*, in addition to her popular *Bridal Call*, both of which are now incorporated into *Foursquare Magazine*, official organ of her "International Church of the Four-square Gospel."

Many people are living today who testify to her practical generosity with food and gifts during grim depression days, yet Sister had her full share of detractors and enemies. She made enemies in the entertainment field when she vigor-ously crusaded against night life in Los Angeles and New York. In Winnipeg, Canada, she surprised that city by visiting the red light district to pray with the "fallen flowers," giving each a colored text to hang in her bed-room. She also incurred much jealousy from certain rival male ministers who failed to match her religious showman-ship and drive and could not compete with her feminine beauty.

Her loudest critic among the Los Angeles clergymen was the Reverend Bob Shuler of Trinity Methodist Epis-copal Church. Mother Kennedy once declared that "No one, except the Lord, was ever persecuted as relentlessly as my daughter." She stressed the fact that Sister had but two enemies in the world that she could recall, "the dance-hall crowd" and "a certain church" (Trinity Methodist Episcopal) where it had been stated in a sermon that "the skids are being put under Angelus Temple."

As Sister's fame spread far and wide, she was deluged with invitations to conduct revivals around the globe. Since she was physically incapable of being everywhere at once, her Bible college, known as the Lighthouse of International Foursquare Evangelism (L.I.F.E.), Inc., trained evangelists, missionaries, and teachers to be sent around the world.

On January 11, 1926, Aimee fulfilled a life-long ambition in visiting the Holy Land and proving to her own satisfaction the accuracy of many Gospel narratives. The truth of Jesus' statement that "a certain man was going down from Jerusalem to Jericho" was impressed upon her when she found it to be downhill all the way! She was even photographed riding a camel, dressed as Isaac's Rebecca.

Returning to California, Sister Aimee, whose life had often been threatened because of her exposeés of corruption, mysteriously disappeared on May 18, 1926, while swimming in the Pacific. Thousands of her congregation maintained a vigil on Ocean Park beach while divers searched for her body. Mrs. Kennedy, now affectionately know as "Ma" Kennedy to the press, wearing a stylish fur-trimmed coat, followed the divers' progress through ear-phones. Concessionaries had a field day selling to the curious composite pictures of Sister rising from the waves. Cecil B. De Mille's masterpiece extravaganza, *The Volga Boat-man*, was premièred the night of Sister's disappearance, but to the studio's chagrin, the story was lost in one of the inside pages. Sister's fate filled the front one!

On Memorial Day, Mother Kennedy held special memorial services at Angelus Temple for her lost daughter. She used the "Light and Darkness" sermon notes that Aimee had left on the beach before entering the fateful water. While the faithful sobbed, an airplane dropped red and white roses over the sea where Sister had last been seen. Thomas Johnson rendered the anthem "Asleep in the Deep."

Los Angeles City Council met in secret session to consider the plea made by a friend of the Temple, Judge Carlos S. Hardy, that permission be granted to bury Sister in a marble crypt beneath her favorite stained glass window.

Commented Mother Kennedy, "She was always taken up by the windows, especially the one portraying Jesus healing the woman. She said she would like to rest under that window."

Unfortunately, the sympathetic council members could take no positive action in amending the ordinance of the city's cemeteries because no body had yet been found. Neither would Coroner Frank Nance grant a death certificate. When it was rumored that the Temple finances were in difficulties (they were actually in excellent order), Mother Kennedy cried, "Oh, why can't they let Sister alone! If the President of the United States had gone in swimming as Sister did, it would be said he drowned!" Sister carried no life insurance, her $300,000 policy having lapsed three months after she had taken it out only the August before. By this time two men had died searching for the body.

Then, notes demanding $500,000 ransom for Sister's return started to reach her distraught mother. They were signed with such crime-fiction nom de plumes as *The Avengers* and the *Revengers*. The former told Mother that if she did not pay up they would "sell her (Sister) to old Felipe of Mexico City." They added as a postscript, "We are sick and tired of her infernal preaching, she spouts scripture in answer to everything."

Mother Kennedy, however, was convinced that Aimee was dead, and diligently went about arranging a last farewell. The congregation of mourners numbered some 17,000 persons. At the evening service, Mother declared that Aimee's empty chair would remain permanently empty.

After that, Sister might well have rested in peace, wherever she might have been; but at 7:30 A.M., on the morning of June 23, Captain Herman Cline of the Los Angeles police awakened Mother with the startling news that he had received word her "drowned" daughter had turned up in Arizona or Mexico. She had escaped from her kidnappers! Mother pulled her robe close to her body. "I don't believe it," she grumbled. "I just can't believe it!"

Then the telephone rang. The voice at the other end came from Douglas, Arizona. It was undeniably Aimee.

The night before, a distraught-looking female had appeared at the front door of Frederick Conrad Schansel, a slaughterhouse keeper who lived a mile and a half from Agua Prieta, Sonora, Mexico. Awakened by his barking dogs, Schansel greeted her in his underwear. She requested help, but while he had gone indoors to put on his pants, she disappeared.

Ramon R. Gonzales, owner of the O. K. Bar, was the next to encounter the mysterious woman, when she appeared at the window of his home, also in Agua Prieta, asking for help. He dressed hurriedly, but his wife, Theresa, found the woman lying, apparently unconscious, by the pathway. Said Theresa, "I think the Senora is dead!"

At 3:00 A.M., the stranger was recovering on the front

porch of the Gonzales home. Through a taxi driver hastily summoned as interpreter, the woman informed them that she was Aimee Semple McPherson.

Later in Douglas, she informed the police that she had been kidnapped back at Echo Beach, having left the water apparently unobserved. She had been accosted by a black-haired woman called "Rosie" who said that her baby was dying and that she would be "ever so happy" if Sister would come over and pray for it. According to Aimee, Mother Kennedy had told them she would.

Sister had then, by her own account, been enticed to a waiting motor car. She was pushed into it, and a sponge filled with a sickly substance was pressed to her nose. The next thing she remembered was coming to her senses in a small room, watched over by the husky Rosie and two male accomplices, one of whom she called Steve. The unidentified man told her she was being held for ransom. . . . "You've taken enough of our girls, and turn about is fair play," he snarled. Sister thought him to be a white slaver. Later, she had a rug thrown over her head and was driven for what seemed hours to a desert shack. Threat followed threat. At one point they threatened to cut off her finger to send Mother Kennedy, who, because of the scar on the tip, would recognize it immediately. An aged man named Felipe appeared, and the kidnappers said that if the ransom they were asking was not paid by her mother, she would be sold to him. Then the men disappeared. Finally, Rosie went shopping for supplies, giving Sister a heaven-sent opportunity to cut herself free from the ropes and straps that bound her by rubbing them against the jagged edge of a tin can. Then she jumped out of the window, and walked for help through the night, on blistered feet.

"I went on and on until I saw a glow in the sky and

thought it must be a village or a town. It looked like Heaven in the distance. I saw lights flashing. Finally I saw a shadow, and as I approached it, I saw it was a building. Habitation at last! A man came out, attracted by the barking of his dogs. He was dressed in BVDS. I begged him to help me."

Aimee was welcomed back to Los Angeles with much rejoicing. As her train drew into the station, the Fire Department band (Sister had once been made an honorary battalion chief after preaching a sermon garbed as a fireman, entitled, "Fireman, Save My Child!") played "Praise God from Whom All Blessings Flow." She was carried to her waiting car sitting in a wicker chair borne on the shoulders of four stalwart firemen. The faithful strewed flowers in her path. Ten minutes after reaching Angelus Temple, she appeared before a congregation of almost six thousand people, and related to them the story of her kidnapping.

Unfortunately, the Los Angeles District Attorney and others not of her flock were skeptical of Sister's story. They alleged that for a woman who had crossed the desert on foot she bore little evidence of hardship. The shack she described could not be found. Some thought she was a mysterious "Miss X," a woman apparently bearing an amazing resemblance to the evangelist who, during part of the time Sister was missing, had been staying in a honeymoon cottage at popular Carmel-by-the-Sea.

One of the Los Angeles papers took to verse on her behalf:

> While I hold no brief for Aimee,
> I'm admitting, all the samee,
> That she might have "rose" alrighty,
> Like another Aphrodite,

> From the deep where she lay soaking
> For a month or two—no joking!
> Then again I haven't tracked her
> From the hut wherein they shacked her,
> Where fair Rosie gagged and tied her,
> With that two-edged can beside her. . . .

A grand jury investigation was instituted, with both Sister and Mother Kennedy being brought to court. Never before had such a three-ring circus appeared in a Los Angeles Court. Only Sister appeared unruffled. After a rugged day in court she would return to preach in her Temple. Even her enemies had to admit she had courage. Doggedly, the Reverend Bob Shuler, his arms upraised like a pugilist, called the kidnapping episode "an outrage against Christianity."

For eighty-eight consecutive days, the name "Aimee Semple McPherson" was blazoned on the front pages of the nation's press. The strain, both physical and mental, of a court investigation to determine whether or not Sister had indeed been kidnapped would have felled a lesser woman, but not Sister. She continued her work without a breach, preparing her evening's sermon while the witnesses were testifying. At last, from her Los Angeles parsonage window, she had the satisfaction of hearing the newsboys cry, "Read all about it—Aimee wins!"

The rest of Sister's life was devoted to evangelism. Like David of the Old Testament, despite any human frailties or errors in judgment, she truly loved God and pursued with single purpose His service, never reckoning the cost to herself of almost superhuman labors in that service.

In the fall of 1927, she visited Great Britain and spoke in the Royal Albert Hall. The occasion was a personal triumph: Aimee was greeted with all the enthusiasm that was later to be lavished upon Billy Graham. According to the *New York Times* of September 29, 1944, she accomplished this "despite having been denounced by a rival Los Angeles minister [Bob Shuler], then in London, as a 'twentieth century Jezebel' who was 'as dangerous as a man who goes to the schoolhouse to sell poisoned candy.' " His words fell on barren ground; the British didn't believe him.

After that, City Hall, Glasgow; Elim Tabernacle, Carlisle and other mighty auditoriums echoed to the exciting, throaty voice of Aimee Semple McPherson.

Night life in Paris and New York did not ecsape her condemnation, but for the enemies she made, there were always thousands of faithful friends. In 1930 she led some of her people on a pilgrimage to the Holy Land, where she was impressed by the "Holy Fire Service" as she saw it enacted at the Holy Sepulcher. The pageant became an annual Easter Sunrise event in Angelus Temple.

On September 27, 1944, Sister Aimee McPherson was again in Oakland, where she had had the inspiration for naming her church. She was still speaking on her cherished topic, "The Foursquare Gospel," and seemed happy and cheerful when she retired that night. The next morning her son, Rolf, found her dead of a heart attack. She was not quite fifty-four.

Even in death Aimee McPherson was not immune to the skeptics. It was rumored that she had died from an overdose of sleeping pills, although her death certificate disproves it. A close friend said, "Knowing Aimee, even dead she would not be found wearing a chin strap."

No sooner had the headlines flashed the news of her demise than the skeptics were busy proclaiming the end of her church. But they were wrong again. Seventeen years later, the Reverend Leland B. Edwards, Assistant Director of Foursquare Foreign Missions, reported in the November issue of *Foursquare Magazine:*

> Today we have missionaries and missionary work in twenty-seven countries outside of the United States and Canada, in all six continents, and in several islands of the sea. It can truly be said, "The sun never sets on the Foursquare Gospel work." We have 685 churches and 452 meeting places in our foreign missionary program, making a grand total of 1137 in all. These figures are from reports several months old and since then many more churches have been started and organized.

In March, 1961, KRKD, the radio station with which Sister's church had been sharing time for several years, was purchased by the denomination, now broadcasting on a twenty-four hour basis under the call letters KRKD AM-FM.

The Foreign Department of Foursquare World Missions has produced five 16 mm color sound motion pictures in addition to filmstrips of Foursquare missionary accomplishments around the world.

Speaking of the effects of his mother's world-wide revivalism, Dr. Rolf K. McPherson says:

> It is true that my mother's ministry was far-flung and not just restricted to the Los Angeles area. Many of our ministers who have traveled abroad come back with the story that wherever they go abroad they come in contact with individuals who have been influenced through the ministry of my mother . . .
>
> My mother received several ordinations as complimentary expressions of appreciation, but the only one I have heard her refer to of any particular importance was the Baptist under date of March 27, 1922, in San Jose, Cali-

fornia. I believe she was also ordained by the Full Gospel Assembly of 943 W. North Avenue in Chicago on January 2, 1909, but I cannot seem to find a document to substantiate this. She actually considered herself interdenominational rather than connected with any one denomination at that time.

On January 1, 1963, *The Evening Bulletin*, Philadelphia, announced:

Angelus Temple—the church built by evangelist Aimee Semple McPherson and her faithful flock—celebrated its 40th anniversary today with an all-day rally.

Anyone who attended the original dedication was invited to participate by the temple's pastor, Dr. Rolf K. McPherson, son of the founder.

Back in the roaring 1920s, Sister Aimee gathered crowds and headlines matching those of today's evangelist Billy Graham.

Chapter Nine

———————————————

THE ANGEL OF
BROADWAY

——————————————————————

Rheba Crawford

(1898=   )

> "I do not believe that publishers are *only* interested in
> material that presents an evangelist as a religious "sex-
> pot." Anyway, the true story of Rheba's life in no way
> fits such a picture, and I cannot be bothered, no matter
> what the price offered, if a story is to be a "phony."
>   A confidante of Rheba Crawford.

Columnist Walter Winchell christened Rheba Crawford
"The Angel of Broadway." Her work among the unfortunate would fill a volume. She was also known as
"Money-back Rheba," because she always returned to the
donors any money she did not use in her welfare work.

The same fund-raising philosophy has been rigidly maintained throughout her career, including those years spent
as California's Director of Welfare. She would not remain

silent if she believed welfare gifts were being misused or wasted—a trait that led her into several bitter battles.

Rheba Crawford was born on February 14, 1898, in Milwaukee, Wisconsin. When she was two years of age the family moved to Sacramento, California, where shortly afterwards her mother died. Rheba's early childhood was spent in close association with her father, Colonel Andrew Crawford, of the Salvation Army. Her earliest memories are of her father spreading his handkerchief so that she might sit on the edge of a wooden sidewalk or on the ground close to the big bass drum while he conducted an outdoor meeting. She was born, reared and trained in active Salvation Army work, and so deep and lasting was the influence of her father's teachings and philosophy upon her life that one can best explain her intense dedication and militant spirit by describing Colonel Crawford. One of his associates described his face as having "Strength and benign dignity mingled with gentleness, a tremendous depth of understanding of human frailties, courage and forgiveness."

As a schoolgirl Rheba was sometimes taunted by thought-less children who followed her home, shouting, "Salvation Army, save my soul!" or other less charitable remarks. On such occasions she would dash into the house, fling her books in one direction, her hat in another, and rush in tears to her father.

"Stop that crying!" was his reaction. "Stand to attention —heels together! You come of fighting ancestors. You are a soldier." Then, gathering her into his arms, he would tell stories of the heroes of the early Salvation Army, their struggle against great odds, their fearlessness and individual triumphs.

Thus it was that she inherited her father's militant Irish spirit. From him, also, she learned the Social Gospel she preaches. Simply stated, Rheba's "Social Gospel" is the teaching that Christ died to purchase salvation for *all* mankind, and to establish forever the dignity of the individual. It encompasses not only the preaching but the literal application of Christ's great commission to "go into the highways and the byways" and reach all humanity of whatever level. It is a militant gospel of action, openly battling against the forces that destroy the bodies or the souls of men.

Having graduated from the North Avenue Presbyterian School and College in Atlanta, Georgia, Rheba entered the Salvation Army Training College in New York. For a time she was assistant editor of the Army's children's magazine. Then she asked to be assigned to the reactivated New York Corps Number 3, which specialized in street meetings. She supervised and advised preaching groups.

From the training college Rheba was sent to St. Petersburg, Florida, to conduct a series of meetings, her first serious independent preaching effort. She was so successful that the Salvation Army barracks proved too small to contain the crowds, and duplicate meetings were held to accommodate them. It was the tourist season and the city was full of people from all parts of the country.

One local pastor chose to take voluble exception to her meetings. The crowds swarmed to hear him, and then returned to Rheba's next meeting to hear her answer his criticism. Somehow, from the very inception of her evangelistic career, wherever this stormy petrel went, excitement followed. Col. Crawford had never taught her how to march backward!

Returning to New York, Rheba obtained permission to conduct meetings from the side steps of the old Gaiety Theater on 46th Street. There was public resentment at first, with some uncomplimentary razzing from the crowds and a few buckets of water sloshed over her head. As Rheba's Irish anger rose, her determination to continue deepened. That was typical. Despite bitter tears, she marched into the hottest part of the battle. A contemporary declares, "I never could decide whether she cried because she was angry, or was angry because she cried."

During those first meetings, when things were difficult, it was a Catholic priest who came to Rheba's rescue. He told the people to stop harassing her—that after listening to her himself he was inclined to believe that wayward members of his own flock who were in her "congregation" might return to their church better members than before.

As her regular meetings continued, the crowds grew and overflowed the sidewalks into the street, and stood there waiting for her. Broadway's Angel had no need to beat a drum to gather followers. Her audience was a strange mixture. Tailored suits brushed shoulders with tattered garments. A captain of police from the tenderloin district stood side by side with characters whose admitted specialties were outside the law. Theatrical folk, returning from circuit tours, came from their check-in headquarters just down the street to join in the hymn singing. At the close of World War I crowds of discharged soldiers roamed the streets like lost sheep with no place to sleep. Many such a one was indebted to the little street corner preacher, who had persuaded a pool room proprietor to let the boys sleep on his tables after closing hours.

Notorious characters of New York's underworld were among Rheba's staunchest defenders, passing the word to "punks" to let her alone. They were the first to contribute gladly to any fund she might be raising to help the sick or destitute of that half-world of which the prosperous part of the population knew little and cared less. Gamblers, girls from the red-light district, and other so-called "untouchables" drifted in and out of her meetings, often calling upon her for help when in trouble. She took the forgotten ones, the underprivileged, to her heart, and has never lost the feeling of personal responsibility to speak for those who have no other voice to plead their cause.

One night while preaching on the Great White Way, Rheba was arrested for obstructing the traffic. The crowd were so infuriated that they followed her in the paddy-wagon to the police station, where they crashed in the door.

Her good friend Walter Winchell hurried down from the Palace Theater, closely followed by former police Captain Reardon. Obtaining her release, they later escorted her home.

The next morning the charge against her was altered to "disturbing the peace," which was promptly dismissed. The only evidence offered against her attested "that she was waving her arms about while leading the singing of gospel hymns," but an avalanche of publicity inevitably followed, and Salvation Army Headquarters was disturbed.

The Army was her life; the street meetings were her first love. But not wishing to embarrass either her superiors or her father, Rheba Crawford resigned. Not unexpectedly, she received flattering offers from the theater to become an actress. These she refused, only wanting to continue her chosen work.

During the few years immediately following, Rheba, hurt and somewhat disillusioned, tried one outlet after another for her message. She held evangelistic meetings in the South, and worked as a columnist on *The Atlanta Consti-*

tution. A hasty marriage turned out unfortunately. Her husband was Harold Sommers, a good-natured playboy type who enjoyed to the full the so-called "good things of life" that an adequate income can provide but which do not always tend to give domestic tranquillity. The marriage might never have taken place if Rheba had not been sympathetic toward his physical handicap, Harold having been crippled in an auto accident. She had been on her way back to New York when he followed, caught up with her in St. Augustine, and persuaded her to marry him.

Rheba has described him as being "an interesting companion, a brilliant and erratic genius, humorous, a complete extrovert . . . completely interested in his own pleasure and profit." He had a lovely estate in Shore Acres, one of Florida's finest residential districts, overlooking the bayou on one side and the bay on the other. There was a landing pier where his two boats were harbored.

However, all this could not dull the deep-seated compulsion, the very theme of Rheba's life, to be active in her social gospel work. Nor could it dim the indignation she felt toward the need and poverty existing close to the fringes of plenty. Husband or no husband, Rheba simply had to preach. She tried it a few times during the less than five years of her marriage. Unfortunately, it did not exactly fit into the Sommers domestic situation. Finally, after they had talked it over, it was decided that she go to her father in San Francisco while Harold obtained a divorce. This he did—"On the grounds of Rheba's incurable propensity for engaging in evangelistic work." He soon married again.

Once more, Rheba turned to preaching. Invited temporarily to occupy the pulpit of the First Congregational Church, she finally found an outlet for her spiritual need.

The selection of a new pastor was delayed for two years, during which time she preached to capacity crowds.

It was in San Francisco that she met and married Ray Splivale.

When James Rolph, Jr. decided to run for governor of California, he requested that Rheba, now Mrs. Splivale, stump the state in behalf of his candidacy, which she did very effectively. She was no novice at "stumping" broad areas. During World War I she had covered the South selling war bonds with such splendid results that Congress had voted her special recognition for her efforts.

Following his election, Governor Rolph appointed her State Director of Welfare. There was bitter opposition from some quarters to a woman's receiving the appointment. Up to that time only one other woman had ever held a responsible state position in California.

Great pressure was brought to bear upon the governor to substitute a man as welfare director. It was a great disappointment to Rheba, who felt that here she was in a position to put the social and welfare gospel into action. To relieve the tension, she offered her resignation, but the governor refused to accept it. He declared that, from her past record, he felt certain her voice would always be lifted in behalf of the needy and underprivileged, and that he would never want such a voice to be absent from the halls of the State Capitol as long as he was governor. Rheba Crawford agreed to remain at her post, and again the battle was on.

The legislature reacted by adjourning without appropriating funds for welfare administration.

This was rather drastic action, at a time when dark Depression clouds were fast gathering. With the governor's permission, Rheba decided to take her problem before the public via personal appearance and radio, but because of political pressure, she found the doors of one radio station after another closed against her. Finally she appealed to Aimee Semple McPherson's station KFSG, Los Angeles.

Sister Aimee and Rheba had met many years before, in Florida. Driving along the road, the latter had come across the unusual spectacle of a beautiful but tired-looking woman pitching her own gospel tent. Filled with admiration for the lady evangelist who was pounding down stakes with the energy of a man, Rheba spontaneously emptied the contents of her purse into the other woman's lap. She did not learn her identity until later.

Now famous, Aimee repaid the good deed by arranging for Rheba Crawford to preach in her Angelus Temple on Sunday mornings and have the use of its radio and radio technicians for her own welfare message on Tuesday evenings.

Sister Aimee preached a strongly evangelistic gospel, for her early roots, too, were in the Salvation Army, and practical service to the unfortunate was an integral part of her ministry. There was no divergence in the preaching message of the two women.

One of the most active departments of Angelus Temple was the Commissary, which gathered in and dispensed food and clothing. It offered a further outlet for Rheba's welfare activities. She coordinated it with the county and city welfare offices so that the Temple could provide immediate food for those in dire distress, yet avoid unnecessary duplication of organized welfare efforts. Although the public welfare personnel worked tirelessly night and day during the worst days of the Depression, the department could not always respond instantly to every call. Orderly records were a necessity, but if a baby was crying for milk (and many were in those days) even a few hours seemed an eternity. So it was arranged that Sister Aimee's Temple Commissary should help fill that gap.

When Aimee's health became seriously impaired, requiring more time from Miss Crawford in the pulpit, the dust of battle over state welfare funds and their administration had settled, leaving Rheba free to preach for the Temple.

Today, Rheba Crawford, militant as ever, is devoting her efforts towards the Los Angeles County Senior Citizens' program. In private life Mrs. Lawrence Lambertz, her second husband having died, she still battles for the underprivileged—in her own words, putting her social gospel to "practical, living use."

Chapter Ten

FATHER WILL
PROVIDE

Rev. M. J. Divine
(Better known as Father Divine)

"April 29—the Anniversary of the Marriage of Father and Mother Divine. . . . GOD at that time . . . nineteen hundred and forty-six, took unto Himself legally a Spotless Virgin Bride in wedlock to unite all nations, all languages, all tongues and all peoples together, to bring an abolition to all division! Not to propagate self-indulgence, sex-indulgence, human affection nor lust and passion, neither races, creeds nor colors, but to propagate Virtue, Holiness, Virginity and Truth and to continue to reproduce it just as I have it between Myself and My Spotless Virgin bride today, the same as She was the day She first stood by My Side!"

"Here's the Answer," 4/22/50 by Father Divine

Father Divine, founder of the worldwide Kingdom of Peace, with thousands of followers in America, Europe, Africa and Australia, is one of the most extraordinary evangelical personages of this or any other generation. A five-foot two-inch colored man, he is God to his devotees.

"I was combusted one day in 1900 on the corner of Seventh Avenue and 134th Street in Harlem," he is quoted as saying when questioned concerning the mysteries of his origin. *The New York Times* of November 18, 1962, added that "nonbelievers say he came into life as George Baker, son of a sharecropper, born near the Savannah River on a Georgia rice plantation about 1880."

The same news story quotes Austin Norris, secretary of Philadelphia's Board of Tax Revision, and Father Divine's lawyer, as declaring, "George Baker is the name given him by his enemies."

Speaking of the flourishing Peace Mission Movement established by Father Divine about forty-five years ago, Norris noted, "The followers have exceptional security. No Divineite fears the future. It is easier to get employment through the Divine organization than any other employment agency in the United States. They can get a high wage because people have high confidence in them, know they are honest."

This is a well-known fact. It is a rare thing for a member of Father Divine's interracial movement to become involved with the police in any way.

With Mother Divine by Father's side, the two work unceasingly together in their cause for international peace.

"I am their life's substance!" Father Divine has said, speaking of his followers. "I am their energy and ambition. They recognize my deity as that which was in the imaginary heaven, and if they can only get a word with me, they feel like they are in heaven."

These followers he has gathered from all walks of life. Many are educated professional men and women—doctors, registered nurses, office workers, teachers and engineers. Society women have been known to forsake their former luxurious lives to become his angels.

Father first came to the public notice when, just prior to 1920, he purchased a twelve-room frame house in a predominantly middle-class white area at 72 Macon Street, Sayville, Long Island. This became the headquarters for him, his first wife, Peninah, and what at first were only a handful of disciples.

In spite of the industriousness of the Divine followers, plus the large amounts that they paid in cash to local storekeepers for their food, they were unpopular in Sayville. White residents thought that the town would soon be filled with Negroes and they would have to sell their properties at a low price. When busloads of people came on Sundays to enjoy the lavish free banquets, the fears of the other Sayville residents seemed to be realized. They had to admit, however, that the leader himself was a quiet and courteous man.

During 1930 several prominent and wealthy white women were converted. Father Divine's fame grew. So did his congregations. "The House of Joy" on Macon Street, where all intoxicating beverages were barred, beckoned larger crowds than ever. Macon Street neighbors objected to the audible praying and singing. Leading citizens organized themselves into a committee to ask Father Divine to move elsewhere. When he politely refused, other tactics were employed. Rumors were fanned that Father was financed by "capitalists," including John D. Rockefeller, who, by feeding the masses, sought to prevent them from open revolt. Mysterious money gifts from people he did not know began to arrive at "The House of Joy." They were sent by neighbors, hoping that Father would accept them and possibly become liable to charges of using the mails to defraud. But Father Divine promptly returned each gift with a simple note saying, "God will provide."

A female detective from New York City was planted among the other angels to report any fraud or evidence of immoral living practiced in "The House of Joy." She failed to find any grounds for complaint, noting instead that even destitute people were always welcome, food and clothing being provided for them.

Thwarted in their desire to get rid of Father, the Sayville committee then used their community influence to have him arrested as a public nuisance.

Not only the Negro press but the white press gave much coverage to Father Divine's appearance in court. In a dignified voice he told the Justice that both the Constitution of the United States and the Declaration of Independence were being "spotted black as my patent leather shoes" by the unfair charge. Sayville received much unfavorable publicity that it had never wanted, while Father Divine acquired national importance. He was pictured as a martyr.

The trial records are amazing. It is hard to believe that such accusations could be made within a few miles of New York City. The Bill of Particulars accusing Father read as follows:

> Defendant claimed to be the Messiah returned to earth; conducted so-called religious services, at which services colored and white people did congregate and mingle together in large numbers; and did then and there encour-

age, aid, and assist those present in shouting and singing in loud tones, annoying neighbors in the vicinity of the defendant's place.

And did then and there permit and encourage large numbers of people on foot and in autos to gather round his place in the highways in and about his place; and did encourage said singing, shouting, exhorting, and stamping to continue past midnight, keeping them awake at all hours of the night and morning.

On May 24, 1932, Father Divine was brought to trial before Supreme Court Justice Lewis J. Smith at Mineola, Long Island. The press recorded that unusual antagonism was shown by the judge toward the defendant. Promptly ordering Father's bail canceled, he had him jailed throughout the trial. Frequently, the judge questioned defense witnesses himself. When a female disciple said, "Peace, Peace, Father," the judge bellowed,

"No! No peace! Just answer the questions."

When Judge Smith asked a white secretary named Helen Faust if she believed Father to be God, she said, "Yes, sir, I do."

He then questioned as to what salary she received. "I don't receive any salary, your Honor," she replied. "I live and board in heaven and get the clothes I need. I'm working for the cause."

"What cause?" demanded Judge Smith.

"Peace and the Brotherhood of Man," replied Miss Faust.

This was too much for the judge. He decided that she didn't look to be the twenty-six years of age she claimed to be (which she was). Turning to his stenographer, the judge ordered, "Record this. If we find this girl is under age, the D. A. will know what his duty is in respect to her."

In his summing up, Judge Smith said of Father Divine that "Those who do not believe him to be God are entitled to have their rights protected . . ." and he declared, "one cannot use religion as a cloak for the commission of crime."

The jury then found Father to be guilty as charged but recommended leniency, which the judge failed to exercise. Instead, he sentenced him to a year in jail and a five hundred dollar fine—the maximum penalty.

That was on Saturday. The following Wednesday, Justice Smith, fifty years old, was dead of a heart attack.

Commented Father Divine from his cell, "I hated to do it."

The prisoner was released on bail after being imprisoned for thirty-three days. Later, the Appellate Court declared that he had been tried prejudicially, and it was quick to reverse the unfortunate Judge Smith's decision.

New fame now awaited Father. Hundreds flocked to hear him. These were depression years. Speaking at a "Monster Glory to Our Lord" meeting on June 25, 1932, at Rockland Palace, New York, Father Divine declared, "You may not have seen my flesh for a few weeks, but I was with you just the same. I am just as operative in the mind as in the body. There were many who thought I had gone some place but I'm glad to say I did not go anywhere. I held the key to the jail all the time I was in it and was with you every time you met. They can prosecute me or persecute me or even send me to the electric chair, but they can never keep me from you or stop me from doing good."

The vast congregation rose to give Father the mightiest ovation of his career. "Need you, Father!" they shouted at the top of their lungs.

Father Divine heeded the cries. He forsook unfriendly

Sayville for New York's Harlem. There, in the year 1933, he opened the first Harlem Heaven.

From that time until 1937, Father Divine's well-run organization filled many an empty stomach. It operated several apartment houses and twenty-five restaurants serving good meals for fifteen cents a person. Properties were leased by his faithful followers in New Jersey, Baltimore, Jersey City and Bridgeport. Posters proclaiming the word "Peace" were commonplace in Harlem stores.

Recalling these depression days Father Divine proudly reviews his record.

"Yes," he said, in a press interview, "we had 2500 to 3000 fed daily in our places in 1935 and '34 and 1933—around that time—and about 2500 to 3000 daily in New York City absolutely gratis, as the people that did not have employment—and also thousands, untold thousands, fed at ten and fifteen cents a meal."

Many ministers of other faiths in the locality became jealous of Father's success and ever-growing congregations. One of them, named Sufi Hamid, was extremely critical, threatening to drive him out of New York. Unfortunately, Sufi Hamid, or "Snoofy," never had the opportunity, for he crashed while learning to fly an airplane.

Pronounced Father, "Sufi Hamid opposed me and was supposed to drive me out of New York City. But the first time he went up in his airplane, he fell and was killed instantly. He called himself a great leader. But as he thought himself great and admitted to a desire to destroy me personally, he destroyed himself. They that would rise up in opposition against me from time to time and everyone who will rise, they will be cut down in the same way. When Sufi Hamid, he rose up against me, he went down so quickly, body and all his power was killed immediately with him."

Father's church right from the beginning had a strict ethical code. Believers refrain from visiting the movies or theater. They do not smoke, drink or use cosmetics. There is no obscenity allowed, or undue mixing of the sexes. They may accept no gifts or tips, even at Christmastime.

The New York Times of November 18, 1962, reported,

> In the Peace Mission hotels, married couples are separated. The movement is a massive cooperative, based on the Biblical Last Supper. Its religious fervor is expressed at the banquet table, or at songfests. There is no formal service, no reading of the scriptures, and there are no ministers.

It was at Rockland Palace, the New Star Casino and St. Nicholas Palace, all in New York City, that Father Divine held his famous Righteous Government Convention in 1936. At that time he invited Pope Pius XI and President Franklin D. Roosevelt, neither of whom attended. Senator Robert Ferdinand Wagner of New York promised Father Divine that Vice President John Nance Garner would read the Divine Platform into the Congressional Record. This platform Father Divine had already explained to the Pope in a registered letter. It stated:

> We are not seeking to form another party, neither to run in collision with partisan parties that are in operation, but to release to them and to all that are in authority the high ideals for true partisanism that all parties might take the fundamentals in the text of my Righteous Government platform to serious consideration and act upon them as a significant legislation. Please kindly endorse it to be handed down to your Congregations as a significant

legislation and to be recommended by all of the Catholic people and in all countries under your Advisory.

Father Divine's headquarters might still have been in New York to this day instead of in Philadelphia had it not been for a woman named Faithful Mary whom he had rescued from a life of alcoholism and prostitution. In one of his heavens she was restored to health and her tubercular condition disappeared. After acting as his emissary in California, she repaid him by trying to usurp his authority.

Faithful Mary then appeared in court as a witness for two fallen angels, Onward Universe and Rebecca Grace, who, before they had joined the Peace Movement, had been an ordinary husband and wife known as Thomas and Verinda Brown.

Rebecca Grace claimed that she had given Father Divine property and money amounting to $4,476 which, instead of being put into the "heavenly treasury," she said, had been used in the names of other angels to buy property.

Father Divine vehemently denied the accusation, swearing that all Rebecca Grace had ever given the movement was "a bunch of flowers for the dining room table." His chances of winning the case were excellent until Faithful Mary took the stand. She stated that she had seen candy boxes filled with so much money in Father's office "that it would make Rockefeller jealous."

A judgment for the $4,476, plus costs, was made against Father, which he steadfastly refused to pay, believing himself to be in the right. After that, he moved himself and his Peace Movement Headquarters bag and baggage to Philadelphia. He reminded the city fathers of New York City that "it can go down just like Sodom and Gomorrah did." For the record, Faithful Mary later admitted at a public meeting she had lied about Father. Soon after, in a California hospital, according to W. M. Poise, one of Father Divine's followers in Los Angeles, "she crawled around the floor like a dog and went crazy." Then she died. Rebecca Grace went on relief.

Today in Philadelphia there are more than twenty of Father Divine's well-run missions and schools, where more than five thousand meals are served daily at thirty-five cents a head. Those who haven't the money may eat free. Followers are known by such character-revealing names as "Angel Flash," "Love, Love, Love," "Bunch of Love," "Job," "Patience," and "Miss Charity." On November 18, 1962, the *New York Times* reported that the movement owned property worth some $10,000,000.

"Woodmont—the "Mountain of the House of the Lord," owned by Palace Mission, Incorporated, and dedicated as the country estate of Father and Mother Divine in 1953—is an imposing thirty-two room castlelike mansion built by a millionaire in 1892 at an estimated cost of a million dollars. It stands on the highest point in Montgomery County at an elevation of 475 feet, overlooking a bend in the Schuylkill River. There are seventy-three acres of beautiful grounds and a 25' x 55' outdoor filtered swimming pool.

Father Divine's first wife, Peninah, had "passed," Father revealed, six years before he took, as his second wife, Sweet Angel, the present Mother Divine, on April 28, 1946. The ceremony was performed by the Reverend Albert E. Shadd, in Washington, D. C.

Sweet Angel, a beautiful blonde, had been born Edna Rose Ritchings, the daughter of a well-to-do Vancouver, Canada, florist. Soft-spoken and cultured, with a brilliant mind, she is considered by Father's followers the most "beautiful body that ever breathed." She uses no make-up.

She is said to have written her first letter to Father Divine when she was seven years old. "For me," she says, "life began when I married Father."

Father Divine once declared, according to press reports, that he had elevated Dwight D. Eisenhower to be President of the United States. He proclaimed, "Peace, it is wonderful. General Eisenhower wasn't ashamed to say it. He is tired of the people making fun of me and of 'Peace, it is wonderful.' He did not just say it, but he even heard the soldiers in the army under his jurisdiction making fun of me. He didn't say it but he heard it. That is what stirred him up so, because he knows what I stand for."

Father Divine is as outspoken on other matters. Of race relations he says, "In My immediate assembly we know no race, no creed, nor color. We know that there is no division and we live it and that is the greater part of what causes the so-called prosecutions and persecutions. But as I so often say, if it would be persecutions, prosecutions, or executions for this cause, I AM willing to stand whatsoever may come if GOD wills it for this Great Cause."

Of the welfare problem he has said, "If you would stop and consider what I really mean to this people, you would know I mean more than merely that which may be termed preaching the Gospel to them . . . My true followers will not remain on the Relief if they are true followers of Mine."

Concerning his stand against insurances and social security, he simply explains, ". . . we also declare it to be contrary to our religious conviction to comply with any insurance law, old age compensation or pension security for the future, in the act of mistrusting GOD for the future, by depending on some uncertain riches and security. Many of us have sacrificed our occupation for our religious conviction, so as not to come under the Social Security Law."

Father Divine has also spoken out against Communism. "Can you not see how Communism is out to devour the righteous judgment of the people all over the world! They try to make the poor and the hungry sell their birthright for a mess of pottage. While they offer food to the hungry that they might live, they cause them to serve a power and a principle that is ungodly.

"But I have come to lead all humanity in the Way of Truth, Freedom and Peace, and if the nations under GOD will adhere to MY Supreme Principle of Life, so will Peace and Prosperity flood the land of every nation as the waters cover the sea."

Finally he describes just what is meant by the separation of the sexes in his Peace Movement, describing the stand taken by those of his people known as Rosebuds, Lily-buds, Crusaders and Young Crusaders:

"My true Rosebuds and even the true sisters, Lily-buds, and others, if they are true followers and members of the Kingdom they have no communication with the opposite sex whatsoever, saving on business and that of a strictly business nature; and that is also vice versally required of those that are in the likeness of men!—whether they be Crusaders or whether they be otherwise elderly or older than the young Crusaders, they are required to live a life of virginity, virtue, and holiness; of honesty, of competence and of truth in all they say and in all they do, and dwell in the Secret Place of the Most High and reside under the shadow of the Almighty."

Chapter Eleven

PROPHET OF THE
NEW FRONTIER

Billy Graham

(1918=)

"God has handed the Gospel trumpet to His church, and in our day we have blown it like a Boy Scout practicing with his first bugle. The noise of our solemn assemblies seems to be one uncertain sound after another. One might think that Christians were following some pseudo-Messiah like Napoleon or Lenin or Hitler, so eager are we to apologize for all our shortcomings."

From *Decision*, published monthly by
The Billy Graham Evangelistic Association

Billy Graham, like the leading evangelists who preceded him, is both product and expression of the era in which he lives. Rising from North Carolina's Bible Belt, he has preached to millions of people, including the Queen of England and other heads of state. He has been seen and heard by more individuals than any other evangelist in history.

Through the medium of television the face of Billy Graham has become familiar in homes around the world. Personable, sunburned and blond, he is the very epitome of the late John F. Kennedy's New Frontier. When enthusiastic supporters suggest him as a possible presidential nominee, Billy Graham proudly replies, "I have been called to a higher vocation than the Presidency."

Unlike his predecessors who were content to win for Christ a city at a time, Billy tells his well-organized team that they must save "strategic areas" of the universe from the "immorality of Communism," which he declares to be "the greatest threat to Christianity in history."

He has held major crusades in Africa, Australia, Canada, the Caribbean, England, France, Germany, Holland, Ireland, Japan, Mexico, New Zealand, South America, Sweden and Switzerland, besides his native United States of America.

His Billy Graham Evangelical Association, with headquarters in Minneapolis, includes on its staff—besides Dr. Graham—the founder and president—fifteen associate evangelists, trained musicians and a platform master of ceremonies.

Its official magazine, *Decision*, boasted in 1963 a circulation of 1,350,000. To date, the association's motion picture operation, *World Wide Pictures*, formerly known as the Billy Graham Evangelistic Films Corporation, has produced more than twenty religious documentaries and dramas. Following Graham's famed New York revival of 1957, it produced the successful *Miracle in Manhattan*, with Jinx Falkenburg and Tex McCrary providing the brisk commentary. *Mr. Texas*, advertised as the "first Christian Western," was another hit. Its theme is the life of a sinful cowboy who finds personal salvation at Billy's Fort Worth, Texas, crusade.

Dubbed "Prophet of the New Frontier" by the press, Billy Graham actually adopted the word "crusade," by which his revivals are known, from Dwight D. Eisenhower, whose European operations in World War II were popularly referred to as crusades.

William Franklin Graham, Jr. was born on November 7, 1918, in a two-story white frame house near Charlotte, North Carolina. His father had been born in a log cabin that once stood on the same spot. Billy's grandfather (born aboard the ship upon which his Scottish-Irish parents were emigrating from Ulster) had dairy-farmed in the vicinity. Billy's mother, Morrow Coffey, was of similar descent, and a graduate of Elizabeth College, Charlotte.

A deeply religious woman, Morrow was instrumental in guiding her son into his chosen vocation. As a youngster, six-foot, three-inch Billy wanted to be a baseball star, but he avers, "I became a preacher because God heard my mother's constant prayers."

Like other leading American evangelists during the last hundred years—D. L. Moody, Billy Sunday and Aimee Semple McPherson—Billy started his life on a farm. By the time Billy was nine, the family milk business had so increased in size that the Grahams were able to move into a pleasant brick Colonial house with "real indoor plumbing." Up at three each morning, Billy helped milk seventy-five cows and then deliver the milk to four hundred waiting customers.

At Sharon High School, his friendliness and general good humor made him popular with his classmates. His father was chairman of the school board. Bible study was always an intimate part of the Graham family life. Every morning at the breakfast table Billy, his younger brother and two sisters learned one verse by heart. They prayed together with their parents each evening. Morrow Graham taught Billy to memorize Psalms 90, 91 and most of the Sermon on the Mount. Each day she set aside a short period when, in the privacy of her bedroom, she prayed that Billy, her elder son, might one day become a minister.

On Sundays the family attended Sharon Presbyterian Church, and once Billy got a thrashing from his father for fidgeting during the sermon. The Graham home was located in a part of the American South still noted for its numerous revival meetings. Itinerant evangelists often pitched their tents in the neighborhood during the Depression days when Billy was growing up. Just as often, Billy's parents asked them back to supper, where the boy attentively listened to the stirring tales of conversion told over his mother's corn and grits. He was not aware that this was one part of his mother's over-all plan to vitalize his interest in the preaching field. Vacations spent in the high mountains at Bible camps were another.

At one such revival meeting the child Billy Graham heard the renowned evangelist, Billy Sunday. He silently watched Sunday's contortionist movements, having been warned in advance by his father that if he so much as uttered a sound, Sunday would call him by name.

Billy's favorite revivalist was Cyclone Mack, a tall, lean individual with raven hair. Up and down the platform marched Cyclone, bellowing salvation in a voice worthy of his name.

Sixteen-year-old Billy hit the Sawdust Trail at a revival meeting conducted by Mordecai F. Ham, an ultrafundamentalist. Mordecai's denunciation, "You are a sinner!"

seemed to be directed straight at the lanky blond youngster.

"I was worried about myself," recalls Billy. "It's difficult to describe the experience of conversion. My heart was lifted and I was a different person."

After graduating from Sharon High School at seventeen, Billy and another boy, Grady Wilson, took summer jobs as Fuller Brush salesmen, traveling from door to door with a sample case. One night, because of vermin-infested lodgings, they were obliged to sleep on the sawdust in a revival tent belonging to a Graham family friend, the Reverend Jimmie Johnson, a young evangelist. Sleeping in their undershorts, their precious suits neatly folded over chairs, the boys were awakened by Johnson, who told them he was off to hold a mission service in Monroe County Jail. Never having seen the inside of such a place, the traveling salesmen asked if they might go, too.

After listening as Jimmie Johnson conducted a brief service in the sordid surroundings, Billy was taken by surprise when the evangelist calmly announced that his "friend" would give the testimony.

But Billy Graham rose to the occasion, pointing his finger, for the first time, in the pose that has since become his most characteristic trademark. Perhaps because of his extreme youth and obvious earnestness, the vagrants, drunks and petty thieves gave him their undivided attention. "Jesus died so that He could take your sins upon His shoulders," the Fuller Brush man shouted, that hot Southern afternoon in Monroe County Jail. Today he considers it his first real sermon.

In 1940 Billy Graham received his degree as Bachelor of Theology at the Florida Bible Institute, and was ordained into the Baptist ministry the same year. Later, at Wheaton

College, Illinois, Billy met and married another Bible student, Ruth McCue Bell, daughter of Dr. and Mrs. L. Nelson Bell of Montreat, North Carolina. The wedding took place at the bride's home on August 13, 1943.

Ruth, who declared in *Grit*, May 12, 1963, that she "would rather be married to Billy Graham and have him only part of the time" than any other man she ever met "and have him all of the time," was planning to become a missionary to Tibet. She was born at Tsingkianpu, 250 miles north of Shanghai, where her father, a Presbyterian medical missionary, was in charge of a large hospital. Learning to speak Chinese before English, she was educated in China and Korea. Later, the Japanese invasion forced her parents to return home to their native America. Ruth Graham derives a personal satisfaction from knowing that now, when her husband crusades in Asia, "he affects the lives of more people in a day than I could have done in years." She enjoys reading books on missionary life to her children.

Billy and Ruth have five children. In 1963 Virginia Leftwich, born on September 21, 1943, married Stephen Tchividjian, son of a Swiss financier, described by the Associate Press as being "Graham's most prominent Swiss disciple." The marriage took place at Montreux, Switzerland, where the bride's father gave his daughter away and later officiated at the ceremony.

Ruth Graham has been a great inspiration to her husband. She has also been of real value in the role of his best critic, and when they are separated because of Billy's work, *Grit* reports, she "supports him constantly in prayer and encourages him to give himself daily to the work of the Lord."

Billy and Ruth Graham do not smoke, dance, play cards

or attend the theater. When Billy was a boy, his father once spanked him for chewing tobacco, because such conduct was unbecoming for a boy set apart by his mother to become a preacher.

Ruth Graham's laughter and sense of humor are contagious. The charm of their home on a Montreat, North Carolina, mountaintop owes much to her ingenuity. She found most of the beams and wood paneling for the structure in deserted neighborhood cabins, and she is proud of the fact that her draperies were bought for twenty-five cents a yard. However, Billy had to stop her making lamps out of old bottles, as he declared that none of them worked. The Graham home is described as being part Swiss chalet and part American ranch house.

Although Ruth has plastered the road to their home with signs calling for privacy while Billy "rests"—something he finds hard to do—the Grahams have sometimes been troubled by moonshiners hiding illicit stills in the seclusion of their woods.

Every crusade means loss of weight for Billy, but Ruth puts it back with Southern cooking, which was not easy for her to learn. She was trained—and prefers—to prepare meals Chinese style.

The Graham home is a haven for a menagerie of pets. Ruth once gave a home to a suffolk ram that butted Billy when he wasn't looking.

When Billy is away, Ruth has her hands full raising a family at Montreat, in addition to doing the chores usually relegated to the man of the household, and she can fix an electrical appliance as well as anyone. She dislikes dishwashing, but that problem was solved one day when she was sick and Billy had to do the job. Now the Grahams have a dishwasher.

Once a year, Ruth makes it her business to read the Bible in its entirety, always finding something new to interest her. She carries the Holy Word from room to room as she works, "to lighten the load." Her favorite Old Testament book is Proverbs, of which she enjoys studying a chapter a day.

Ruth does not care for television, while Billy watches only Westerns or the performance of a star who has come to him for counsel.

If he had been able to speak to the cinema actress Marilyn Monroe, her suicide might have been prevented. After her tragic death in 1962, it was revealed that two weeks earlier Billy had awakened in a Seattle hotel "with a burden to pray for her." When the feeling continued, one of the Graham associates tried desperately to reach Miss Monroe through one of her agents, only to be met with a blank wall: "Not now. Maybe two weeks from now." But two weeks was too late.

Billy Graham experienced his first phenomenal successes as a preacher in Los Angeles, Aimee Semple McPherson's home ground in the Roaring Twenties. After doing moderately well as a circuit evangelist from 1943 to 1949, Billy traveled to the West Coast, where, in Los Angeles, "the world's largest revival tent" was awaiting him. He was hoping for a sign from God to tell him whether he should stay in that part of the country, and it came in the surprising form of newspaper publicity directed by William Randolph Hearst, who had ordered his editors to "puff Graham."

Typed as "Gabriel-in-Gabardine," Billy was interviewed by the best of Hearst's team of reporters and columnists. His photographs in what to millions became familiar poses first appeared headlined in the *Los Angeles Examiner* and the *Herald-Express*. There, readers learned of Billy's battle for gangster Mickey Cohen's soul, which was said to have ended in a draw. For a time it seemed to Los Angeles that the breathless days of Sister McPherson's personal ministry had returned.

Billy's next stop was Boston, where he was slated to preach at Park Street Congregational Church. Boston newspapers took up the torch where their Los Angeles counterparts had left off. They found the handsome blond evangelist excellent copy and a sure circulation builder. When 2,500 worshippers failed to get into the church on opening night, Billy was obliged to move to Mechanics' Hall. From there he went on to Boston Garden, where his audience numbered 14,000. Finally, he preached to 50,000 on Boston Common. *Time* and *Life*, Henry R. Luce's magazines, prophesied "a great spiritual awakening."

Billy commented later, "I'll never forget those crowds. Religion wasn't considered news. But when we went to Portland, Maine, the headlines telling of our arrival looked like war had been declared."

The truth was that Billy Graham, Evangelist, was not just a myth created to boost newspaper circulations. A man with a message, he was determined to stay.

With his future as an evangelist now ensured, Billy Graham followed in the footsteps of D. L. Moody when he decided to accept an invitation from more than a thousand clergymen in Britain's Greater London area, whose empty churches proclaimed the need for a revival.

Billy, now a Doctor of Divinity, quietly prepared for the mammoth assignment ahead, unaware that a storm was brewing. The publicity experts sent ahead had done their job a little too thoroughly for the conservative British. Billy's face was everywhere. Even nonchurchgoers openly voiced their resentment, while irate clergymen wrote protesting letters to the newspapers. But worse was to come. Billy was reported to have declared that socialism had done more harm to England than Hitler's bombs.

The word he had really used was "secularism." Although a retraction was immediately made, nobody wanted to listen. Instead, a Labor member of Parliament demanded that Billy Graham be deported as "an undesirable alien."

Billy duly arrived at London's Waterloo Station, accompanied by his wife, who had flatly refused to refrain from using lipstick. This had been Billy's suggestion, as he had heard that many Britishers disliked it. He had already sacrificed his own pistachio-green suits and Bible-emblazoned ties for the least flashy of wardrobes—including a conservative hat. London's famed Harringway Arena had been rented for three months for the Graham Crusade.

Billy had invited two friends, Senators Stuart Symington of Missouri and Henry Bridges of New Hampshire, to be present at the first meeting. On the afternoon preceding the opening night, Symington called Billy with the distressing news that Ambassador Winthrop Aldrich James had advised them not to attend. The criticism of Billy in the British press was given as the reason. Day after day he had been dubbed everything from "a hot gospeler come from God's Own Country to save our souls" to "a surplus American saint."

Clasping each other's hands, Billy and Ruth Graham drove to Harringway Arena to meet their fate. Even the weather seemed against them, snowing, raining and sleeting all at the same time. Earlier, at his hotel, Billy had been informed that there were only a few in the audience other than a battery of three hundred reporters, photographers and newsreel cameramen. When the Grahams reached the entrance they did not see a single person. Billy braced himself to face an empty arena.

But he was wrong: the place was packed. He even found Symington waiting. "While taking a bath," the Senator said, "I couldn't get this meeting off my mind, so I called Senator Bridges and told him that we cannot let Billy down."

If Billy had thought his Boston crowds extraordinary, his first in London was almost unbelievable. Even Anglican bishops were in attendance.

Gripping the edge of the rostrum, Billy Graham began to speak. "We have not come to save London," he began, his voice strangely tender. "We are not here to try to reform you. We can only hope to light a little spark. We have come at the invitation of the leaders of your church to help them bring a spiritual awakening such as you have not had since Wesley."

Next day the press favorably reported his initial meeting. The "undesirable alien" was described by the *Manchester Guardian* as possessing "a holy simplicity." *The Times* called his preaching "far from being in bad taste and alien to the British way."

During the weeks that followed, people flocked from all parts of the British Isles to hear the good-looking American. They numbered more than 1,500,000. The Right Reverend Geoffrey Francis Fisher, then Archbishop of Canterbury, sat by Billy's side when he preached before record crowds at Wembley Stadium. Among the converts, numbered at 23,806, was Sir John Hunt, leader of the expedition that conquered Mount Everest. The House of Commons, which had first questioned his integrity, gave a luncheon and dinner to honor Graham, with Harold MacMillan (later Prime Minister) presiding at the former.

The Grahams never drank so much orange juice in their lives as in England, where they found that even Church of England bishops took sherry or wine of some sort.

Her Majesty Queen Elizabeth, the Queen Mother and the Princess Margaret were among the notables who invited Billy and Ruth Graham to their homes. Princess Margaret, always deeply interested in theology and metaphysics, met the Grahams at Clarence House, the Queen Mother's home.

Winston Churchill also asked to meet Billy, who told Britain's senior statesman "what Christ had done for me and could do for the world."

Billy was invited to Number 10 Downing Street to have an interview with Sir Winston shortly after the experiment with the hydrogen bomb. At that time Britain was tremendously shaken. Sir Winston, then almost pessimistic about the future, commented to the evangelist that "our problems are beyond us." When Billy replied that Jesus Christ was the only hope of mankind in an era such as this, Britain's wartime Prime Minister replied, "Perhaps young man, you may have the answer after all."

Unlike her great-great-grandmother Queen Victoria, Queen Elizabeth II was interested in American evangelists and invited the Grahams to lunch at Windsor Castle. Billy later preached in the private chapel at Royal Lodge, Windsor Park, to Her Majesty, Prince Philip and other members of the Royal Family.

In 1959 and 1961 Dr. and Mrs. Graham were again received by the Queen and Prince Philip at Buckingham Palace, where they had tea.

When Billy preached for six weeks in Glasgow, it was

necessary to reactivate the bomber-alert telephone system that had not been used since World War II so that the sermons could be relayed to waiting congregations in 2,500 cities and towns. Glasgow and Oxford University students debated on the question of whether Graham was an undesirable alien or not. Glasgow won, having taken the negative opinion.

Cambridge University invited the evangelist to preach, which he did, wearing the appropriate robes.

As if this success were not enough, Billy went on to Scandinavia, the Netherlands and West Germany. At Geneva he was on hand for a Big Four Summit Conference, attending church with President Eisenhower and John Foster Dulles. At Eaux Vives Park he spoke to 20,000 people, proclaiming that if God were not made Number One Delegate, the Summit Conference would surely fail.

In France he preached for five nights in the Velodrome s'Hiver. The publication *Le Monde* remarked, "Better bow before the spiritual dynamism of this man, whose formula and phrases are perhaps infantile, but who touches his public."

"I go to New York in fear and trembling," Billy Graham is reported to have said before his assault on the great American metropolis. For weeks he had been preparing for that day.

So had his advance guard.

In 1954 Graham had been asked by the Evangelistic Department of the New York Protestant Council of Churches to revitalize religious life in their churches by means of a gigantic crusade to open May 15, 1957. At that time fifty-seven per cent of New Yorkers were said to have no regular church of their own.

The Graham publicity team was not unlike that used by Billy Sunday when he "conquered" the city back in 1917. However, the costs were higher in hard cash. Graham spent $322,308 for publicity and advertising services alone compared with Sunday's entire budget of $320,000 for a ten-week revival.

Whereas Sunday used famed publicity consultant Ivy Lee to promote him, Billy Graham had Jerry Beavan, known as his executive secretary. A year prior to the actual opening of the crusade, Beavan moved into the heart of the Broadway theatrical district. His office was located on West 46th Street.

As had been the case in the campaigns of Moody and Sunday, influential names appeared on the list of the general crusade committee, including William Randolph Hearst, Henry R. Luce, Norman Vincent Peale and George Champion, president of the Chase Manhattan Bank. Later, an executive committee was formed.

The first task was to interest *all* of New York's Protestant ministers in the revival. For the past two years Billy had made a number of public appearances in the city, and many individual ministers now knew and liked him. There were, however, some dissenters, notably among the clergy of the Protestant Episcopal Church, who were against what they termed "a circus spectacle." Conversions by the hundreds coupled with Billy's literal Bible teaching were not to everyone's taste. One of Billy's quotes was, "I do not believe that God created life and then over a process of many thousands of years it evolved into what we call man." Some twentieth century theologians can agree with his beliefs that the Bible is literally correct and inspired by God Himself.

Several Protestant Episcopal ministers, notably the Reverend Charles Howard Graf, rector of the popular St. John's-in-the-Village, had specific questions to ask concerning the Graham crusade. For one thing, Dr. Graf found it hard to comprehend how Billy could write a daily newspaper column and go through the tensions of conducting a crusade that lasted ninety-seven nights, exclusive of large individual rallies. Dr. Graf well knew, from his own experience, the grinding task of putting out a daily newspaper column while running a parish at the same time.

The repercussions of the Greenwich Village rector's remarks exceeded all expectations. He was deluged with mail from outraged Graham admirers, much of it so vitriolic in content that had Billy been aware of the contents he might well have condemned the writers. A new Jersey woman wrote Dr. Graf that when Billy Graham appeared on television she had seen the Holy Ghost sitting upon one of his shoulders.

The Graham team was busy working with the friendly ministers. One clergyman was told, "Billy is only the obstetrician; you will be the pediatrician." Out of the 3,000-odd Protestant ministers in New York City, 1,500 were willing to be included in the great crusade. Their first job was to arrange their own individual committees.

Willis Haymaker was in charge of recruiting prayer groups to work hundreds of Manhattan's city blocks. Mrs. Norman Vincent Peale took charge of the ten thousand prayer groups he had organized in offices and homes. Graham literature made New York mailmen think they had another Christmas rush to contend with. The *New York Crusade News* was sent free to all who asked for it. No single opportunity was lost. College students, actors, actresses, teenagers, and housewives found themselves invited to join student groups to prepare for Graham's coming and the success of what has since been termed the "greatest revival in history." New York's friendly ministers even contributed the services of 5,000 singers, out of which two choirs of 1,500 each were chosen and trained to sing on alternate nights.

Counselors chosen to deal with the "inquirers" seeking conversion were told to be interdenominational in their approach and use deodorants. The *New York Times* devoted three pages to the revival's opening.

Madison Square Garden could hold 19,000 people. A total of 11,500 seats were taken nightly by church delegations numbering 7,500 members, 1,000 counselors, 500 ushers and 1,500 choir members. Each Saturday evening an additional estimated 8,000,000 to 10,000,000 saw and heard Billy Graham on network television. He attended numerous individual functions connected with the revival, including rallies in Forest Hills and Harlem. Mrs. Cornelius Vanderbilt Whitney gave a lawn party.

In contrast with such vast publicity, the services themselves were noticeably simple, while the singing was outstanding. The *Christian Century* described the venture as being "a strange new junction of Madison Avenue and Bible Belt."

Whereas Billy Sunday's revival statistics revealed an attendance of 1,250,000 persons in ten weeks, Billy Graham's compared favorably, with 1,687,000 in sixteen. Sunday's conversions were numbered at 98,254; Graham's at 56,767. According to published press reports, the crusade cost over $2,500,000, including $1,054,439 used to purchase space for Billy's thirteen Saturday television sermons.

As in London, and indeed after all his Crusades, Billy Graham's converts were all exhorted to attend the churches of their individual choice.

During the crusade Graham's platform was visited by many celebrities, from Ethel Waters, who sang, "Nobody knows the Trouble I've Seen," to Vice-President Richard M. Nixon. The most poignant moment of the entire crusade—and there were many—was when Billy Graham introduced the audience to his mother. Looking out upon that sea of faces, she thought how her prayers that Billy might become a preacher had been answered a thousand-fold.

One of Billy's most valuable assets is his ability to convey his message of salvation to those whose basic language is not English. With the aid of interpreters, his preaching to the crowds was particularly successful in India. He told them that Christianity had been born in Asia; that "Christ's skin was a little lighter than yours and a little darker than mine."

Billy feared that the people clamoring to touch his person were accepting him as a God. Many came on foot and by oxcart from all over Southern India to hear him. Most of his listeners were not Christian.

Graham's quiet, direct approach to the Indian crowds pleased Jawaharlal Nehru, who gave his blessing to the Graham crusade. The Prime Minister had not been impressed when Billy, at the advice of the United States State Department, told him how much Americans liked and admired him, but he was touched by Billy's uninhibited confession of faith.

"Mr. Nehru," Billy said, "when I decided to live for Christ, He changed me. He gave me peace and joy! Before this decision, I didn't care anything about God, the Bible or people. I was filled with intolerance, but the simple act changed my nature. I began to worship God and I loved people no matter what color their skin might be. Christ can do that for everyone!"

In 1963, *Time* magazine reported that "the great post-war religious revival in the U. S. is over—and many church leaders are thankfully saying 'Amen,' " but the message of Billy Graham is far from dead.

During a debate in Britain's House of Commons concerning the relationship between Parliament and the established Church of England, a Conservative member, J. H. Cordle, declared that "the religious life of England today owes far more to Dr. Billy Graham than to many of the bishops!"

Governor John B. Connally, Jr., of Texas, commented, "In a time of cold war, many of us have many problems, some small and some great. It is a matter of profound gratitude to me that we have in this land and in this world men like Dr. Billy Graham. I know of no man of this time who has meant more to the people of this world, from India to Australia, in bringing inspiration, hope and understanding to them, and reaffirmation of faith to free peoples with free souls throughout the world . . . I give thanks that we have men like Dr. Billy Graham to remind us constantly of our own smallness and of our own weaknesses, and to remind us everlastingly of our need for devotion to God."

Decision, the monthly magazine of the Billy Graham Evangelistic Association—two and a half years old in May, 1963—published French and German language editions to coincide with Graham crusades in those countries.

During the early part of 1963, Billy was forced to cancel a personal role in the Philippine Islands Crusade, and fears for his health were expressed by well-wishers throughout the world. His illness was attributed to a "very strange virus that seemed to move from one part of his body to another." Contributing in a major way to this physical condition were years of overwork.

However, on April 17, a tin-hatted Billy was back in harness to shovel out the first spadeful of earth for the Billy Graham Pavilion at the New York 1964-1965 World's Fair.

Speaking to the official dignitaries, workmen and others gathered on that occasion, Billy declared:

". . . We have accepted the invitation of the World's Fair officials to build an evangelistic pavilion where we can present the Biblical message with an evangelistic emphasis that has characterised our ministry. We do not intend to duplicate the efforts of others.

"The pavilion will be unique and different! In its presentation of Biblical truth it will use every modern technique that science can provide.

". . . We intend to minister to all races and all cultures. There will be various rooms within the pavilion dedicated to nearly every part of the world.

"As the thousands of visitors pour through these gates in 1964 and 1965 to attend the greatest Fair in modern history, they will be reminded of the moral and spiritual strength that lies at the foundation of our republic.

"Man stands at the crossroads of eternity. A decision of vast preparation must soon be made by the human race. Will it be the road to war and destruction, or the road to peace? We are approaching the threshold of a materialistic paradise on earth, created by science, or alternately, a hell so terrifying that the human mind cannot comprehend it. We are hopeful that this pavilion will make some small contribution in helping the world to choose God and peace."

Bibliography

SELECTIVE BIBLIOGRAPHY

Chapter 1   Wesley and Whitefield

JOHN WESLEY

Dictionary of National Biography, Vol. LX, Sidney Lee, ed. London, 1899.

Johnson, Samuel, *The Letters of Samuel Johnson*, ed. G. B. Hill, ed. Oxford, 1892.

Kroll, Harry Harrison, *The Long Quest: the Story of John Wesley*. Philadelphia, 1954.

The Moravians and Wesley—Charleston, 1949.

Pennington, Edgar Legare, *John Wesley's Georgia Ministry*. Pamphlet, Chicago, 1939.

Rowden, Alfred W., *The Primates of the Four Georges*. New York, 1916.

Sherwin, Oscar, *John Wesley, Friend of the People*. New York, 1961.

Terry, Benjamin, *A History of England For Schools*, Chicago, 1904.

Tyerman, the Reverend Luke, *The Life and Times of John Wesley*, 3 vols. New York, 1872.

Wesley, John, *The Works of John Wesley*, 7 vols. New York, 1831.

Wesley, John, *Journal*, 4 vols. London and New York, 1930.

Wesley, John, *Sermons on Several Occasions*, 3 vols. New York, 1831.

Wesley, John, *The Letters of John Wesley,* ed. John Telford, 8 vols. London, 1931.

Wesley, John, *An Extract from Milton's Paradise Lost.* London, 1769.

Wesley, John, *Primitive Physic: An Easy and Natural Method of Curing Most Diseases.* Many editions published during Wesley's Lifetime in England and America.

Wesley, John and Charles, *The Poetical Works of John and Charles Wesley,* 13 vols. London, 1870.

Wood, G. Bernard, "Past Recalled in Northern Churches," Article, *Country Life Magazine,* p. 497, Feb. 28, 1963.

Young, Arthur, *A Six Weeks' Tour,* London, 1769.

Young, Arthur, *Travels in France during the Years 1787, 1788, 1789.* London, 1924.

Both the British Museum and the New York Public Library have excellent card index references pertaining to John Wesley. In addition, the following are to be found in the Georgia Historical Society headquarters, Savannah, Georgia:

Colonial Records of the State of Georgia, The, A. D. Candler, ed. Atlanta, 1904-1916. 26 vols. plus 13 unpublished, typed vols.

Coulter, E. M., *When John Wesley preached in Georgia.* Savannah, Georgia Historical Society, 1925.

Gamble, Thomas, *The Love Stories of John and Charles Wesley.* Savannah, Pub. by the author, 1927.

Pennington, E. L., *John Wesley's Georgia Ministry.* Reprinted from *Church History,* vol. III, no. 3, Sept. 1939.

Percival, Diary of Viscount, afterwards First Earl of Egmont. London, His Majesty's Stationery Office, 1920. Vols. 2 and 3.

Journal of the Rev. John Wesley, A.M., The, Nehemiah Curnock, ed. London, 1909 and 1938. Vol. 1.

GEORGE WHITEFIELD

Andrews, J. R., *George Whitefield.* Sovereign Grace Union Publication, No. 183. 1930.

Belden, Albert David, *George Whitefield—the Awakener.* Nashville, 1931.

Butler, Dugald, *John Wesley and George Whitefield in Scotland.* Edinburgh and London, 1898.

Cross, Arthur Lyon, *The Anglican Episcopate and the American Colonies.* Cambridge, Mass., 1924.

Edwards, *The Select Works of Jonathan* (3 volumes), The Banner of Truth Trust, London, 1958, 1959, 1961.

Henry, Stuart C., *George Whitefield—Wayfaring Witness.* Nashville MCMLVII.

Newly Discovered Letters of George Whitefield, 1745-46, edited by John W. Christie. Journal of the Presbyterian Historical Society, XXXII, Nos. 2-4, pp. 69-90; 159-186; 241-270; June-December, 1954.

Whitefield, George, *The Works of the Reverend George Whitefield.* 6 vols. London 1771-2.

Whitefield's Journals, to which is Prefixed His "Short Account" and "Further Account." William Wale, ed. London, 1905.

Dictionary of National Biography. Vol. LXI. Edited by Sidney Lee, London, 1900.

Chapter 2

JOHN LEWIS DYER

Colorado Magazine, The, July 1958, pp. 196-197. Contains description of "Father" Dyer.

Collier, William R. and Edwin V. Westrate, *Dave Cook of the Rockies.* New York, 1936. Contains information on Reynolds Gang and the gold dust delivered by "Father" Dyer which was lost in the Buckskin Coach holdup.

Cook, David J., *Hands Up: A Pioneer Detective in Colorado,*
(Autobiography). Denver, 1897.
De Voto, Bernard, *The Course of Empire.* Boston, 1952. Con-
tains data on Lt. Zebulon Montgomery Pike. pp. 423, 425,
427, 431.
Dyer, John Lewis, *The Snow-Shoe Itinerant* (Autobiography).
Cincinnati, 1890.
Ghost Towns of Colorado, pp. 13-30. Chapter "Pike's Peak or
Bust!" American Guide Series. New York.
Hall, Gordon Langley, *The Two Lives of Baby Doe.* Phila-
delphia, Macrae Smith, 1962. pp. 15-17. Contains details
of Pike's Peak Gold Rush. pp. 29-34. "Father" Dyer in
Buckskin Joe.
Kraus, Michael, *The United States to 1865.* Allan Nevins and
Howard M. Ehrmann, eds. p. 469. "Pike's Peak or Bust."
Ann Arbor, Michigan. 1959.
Muzzey, David Saville, *A History of Our Country.* Boston,
1946. Contains data on Zebulon Montgomery Pike.
Willison, George F., *Here They Dug the Gold.* London, 1950.
Both the Colorado State Museum and the Western History
Department, The Public Library, the City and County of
Denver, have excellent files of background material in-
cluding photographs, of "Father" Dyer's era.
Zilch, John H., *Memorial to "Father" John L. Dyer. Colorado
Magazine,* Vol. XL. #3 (July, 1963).

Chapter 3

DWIGHT L. MOODY

Barnwell, R. Grant, *The Life of Moody and Sankey, the
American Evangelists,* Philadelphia, 1875.
Boyd, Robert, *The Wonderful Career of Moody and Sankey
in Great Britain and America.* New York, 1875.

Bradford, Gamaliel, *D. L. Moody: A Worker in Souls*, New York, 1927.

Chapman, J. Wilbur, *The Life and Work of Dwight L. Moody*, New York, 1900.

Covert, William C., *Dwight L. Moody*. The Northfield Schools, 1937.

Curtis, Richard K., *They Called Him Mister Moody*. New York, 1962.

Davis, George T. B., *Dwight L. Moody: The Man and His Mission*. Chicago, 1900.

Day, Richard Ellsworth, *Bush Aglow*. Philadelphia, 1936.

Moody, Paul D., *My Father*. Boston, 1938.

Moody, William R., *The Life of Dwight L. Moody*, New York, 1900.

Pollock, J. C., *Moody*. New York, 1963.

Powell, Emma Moody, *Heavenly Destiny: The Life Story of Mrs. D. L. Moody*. Chicago, 1943.

Chapter 4

RODNEY SMITH

Smith, Rodney, *Gypsy Smith: His Life and Work*. London, 1904.

Chapter 5

BILLY SUNDAY

"Billy Sunday, Prophet or Charlatan." Article, *Overland Monthly*, San Francisco, Vol. 71 (1918), pp. 75-80.

Brown, Elijah P., D.D., *The Life and Work of Reverend William Ashley Sunday, D.D., The Baseball Evangelist*. New York, 1914.

Ellis, William Thomas, *"Billy" Sunday: the man and his message, with his own words, which have won thousands for Christ*. Philadelphia, 1914. (A further edition published in 1936 contains Mr. Sunday's autobiography, a concluding chapter by Mrs. William A. Sunday, and a yoke-fellow's tribute by Homer A. Rodeheaver. Also words and music of "De Brewer's Big Hosses.")

Frankenberg, Theodore Thomas, *Billy Sunday, His Tabernacles and Sawdust Trails: a biographical sketch of the famous baseball evangelist*. Columbus, Ohio, 1917.

McLoughlin, William G. Jr., *Billy Sunday was His Real Name*. University of Chicago, 1955.

Rodeheaver, Homer A., *Song Stories of the Sawdust Trail*. Foreword by the Rev. William A. Sunday. New York, 1917.

Sunday, William Ashley, *Mother's Sermon*. Sturgis, Mich. 1909.

Sunday, William Ashley, *Burning Truths from Billy's Bat* (Epigrams). Philadelphia, 1914.

Sunday, William Ashley, *Billy Sunday Speaks* (Epigrams). Grand Rapids, Mich., 1937.

Sunday, William Ashley, *Wonderful* (Epigrams). Winona Lake, Indiana. (Undated).

Sunday, William Ashley, *Autobiography. Ladies' Home Journal*, 1932-3.

Wright, Melton, *Giant for God*. Boyce, Virginia, 1951.

Obituary, *New York Times*, November 7, 1935.

Chapter 6

EVANGELINE BOOTH

Wisbey, Herbert A., Jr., *Soldiers Without Swords—A History of the Salvation Army in the United States*. New York, 1955.

Wilson, Philip W., *General Evangeline Booth of the Salvation Army*. New York, 1948.

Booth, Evangeline and Hill, Grace Livingston, *The War Romance of the Salvation Army*. Philadelphia, 1919.

Ervine, St. John, *God's Soldier: General William Booth*. Vols. I and II. New York, 1935.

Begbie, Harold, *Life of William Booth: The Founder of the Salvation Army*. Vols. I and II. London, 1920.

Chapter 7

DADDY GRACE

See newspaper quotations as noted in this chapter for further source material.

Chapter 8

AIMEE SEMPLE McPHERSON

Browne, Lewis, *This Believing World*, New York, 1926.

Bridal Call, Aimee Semple McPherson, ed. Weekly publication, Los Angeles, 1927-1934.

Edwards, Rev. Leland B. (Assistant Director of Foursquare Missions), "Our Foreign Missions Program: a Comprehensive View." *Foursquare Magazine*, November, 1961.

"Exploits of Sister Aimee in Roaring Twenties Recalled." *The Evening Bulletin*, Philadelphia, Jan. 1, 1963, p. 5B.

Medal for Sister, A, In Memoriam, Aimee Semple McPherson 1890-1944, pub. approx. 1944 by Four Square.

McPherson, Aimee Semple, *Give me my own God*, New York, 1936. Published in England as *I Viewed the World*.

McPherson, Aimee Semple, "The Herald Angels." *Foursquare Magazine*. Dec., 1962 (Published posthumously).

McPherson, Aimee Semple, *In the Service of the King: The Story of My Life*, New York, 1927.

McPherson, Aimee Semple, *The Story of My Life, 1890-1944.* In Memoriam. With foreword by her son Rolf K. McPherson, D.D. Los Angeles, 1951.

McPherson, Aimee Semple, *The Story of My Life.* In Memoriam. Los Angeles, Echo Park Evangelistic Association, 1951.

McPherson, Aimee Semple, *This is That.* Personal Experiences, Sermons and Writings of A. S. McPherson, Evangelist. Los Angeles, Cal., Echo Park Evangelistic Association, 1923.

Chapter 10

FATHER DIVINE

Father Divine—His Words of Spirit Life and Hope, St. John Evangelist and James Hope, eds. Published by Father Divine, 1961.

Here's the Answer containing typical questions asked concerning Father and Mother Divine and the Peace Mission Movement, etc.

"Father Divine is Extending 'Kingdom of Peace.' " *New York Times*, Sunday, November 18, 1962, p. 124.

Chapter 11

BILLY GRAHAM

Burnham, George, *Billy Graham: a Mission Accomplished.* Westwood, N.J., 1955.

Burnham, George, *To the Far Corners with Billy Graham in*

Asia, including excerpts from Billy Graham's Diary. Westwood, N.J., 1956.

Cook, Charles Thomas, *The Billy Graham Story: One Thing I Do.* Wheaton, Illinois, 1954.

Cook, Charles Thomas, *London Hears Billy Graham.* With Foreword by Hugh R. Gough. London, 1955.

Colquhoun, Frank, *Harringay Story:* The official record of the Billy Graham Greater London Crusade. London, 1954.

Crusade in Scotland, Tom Allan, ed. London, 1955.

Graham, William Franklin, *Calling Youth to Christ.* Includes Introduction by Torrey M. Johnson. Grand Rapids, Michigan, 1947.

Graham, William Franklin, *My Answer.* Garden City, N.Y., 1960.

Graham, William Franklin, *The Secret of Happiness.* Garden City, N.Y., 1955.

High, Stanley Hoflund, *Billy Graham: The Personality of the Man, His Message and His Mission.* New York, 1956.

Mitchell, Curtis, *God in the Garden: the story of the Billy Graham New York Crusade.* Garden City, N.Y., 1957.

DISCARDED

DATE DUE